The End
of the Novel
# of Love

ALSO BY VIVIAN GORNICK

Approaching Eye Level

Fierce Attachments

The End of the Novel of Love

VIVIAN GORNICK

Beacon Press

Boston

BEACON PRESS
25 Beacon Street
Boston, Massachusetts 02108-2892

BEACON PRESS BOOKS
are published under the auspices of
the Unitarian Universalist Association of Congregations.

Printed in the United States of America

03 02 01 00 99 98   8 7 6 5 4 3 2

Text design by Anne Chalmers
Text composition by Wilsted & Taylor

Library of Congress Cataloging-in-Publication Data
Gornick, Vivian.
The end of the novel of love / Vivian Gornick.
p. cm.
ISBN 0-8070-6222-7 (cloth)
ISBN 0-8070-6223-5 (paper)
1. Love stories, American—History and criticism.   2. Love stories, English—History
and criticism.   3. Women and literature—United States—History.   4. Women
and literature—Great Britain—History.   5. Man-woman relationships in
literature.   6. Women in literature.   7. Closure (Rhetoric)   I. Title.
PS374.L6G67   1997
813'.08509352042—dc21   97-10490

☞ Contents ☜

Diana of the Crossways

IN A THOUSAND NOVELS of love-in-the-Western-world the progress of feeling between a woman of intelligence and a man of will is charted through a struggle that concludes itself when the woman — at last — melts into romantic longing and the deeper need for union. There are, however, a handful of remarkable novels written late in the last century and early in this one — among them *Daniel Deronda, The House of Mirth, Diana of the Crossways, Mrs. Dalloway* — where, at the exact moment the woman should melt, her heart unexpectedly hardens. Just at this place where *give* is required, some flat cold inner remove seems to overtake the female protagonist. In the eyes of the world she becomes opaque ("unnatural" she is called), but we, the privileged readers, know what is happening. The woman has taken a long look down the road of her future. What she sees repels. She cannot "imagine" herself in what lies ahead. Unable to imagine herself, she now thinks she cannot act the part. She will no longer be able to make the motions. The marriage will be a charade. In that moment of clear sight sentimental love, for her, becomes a thing of the past. Which is not to say the marriage will not take place; half the time it will. It is only to say that in these novels this is the point at which the story begins.

The response of these intelligent fictional women—Gwendolen Harleth, Lily Bart, Diana Warwick, Clarissa Dalloway—to the prospect of married love goes against the grain. Not only because we all know that love is the most formative experience a human being can have and marriage, any marriage, at least in its beginnings, reminds one of its promise, but also because the idea that a woman, any woman, could really want anything other than to be safely settled in the world with a husband has, until very recently, been unthinkable.

So what is it with Gwendolen, Lily, Clarissa, and Diana?

In *Daniel Deronda* George Eliot pits the beautiful Gwendolen Harleth (shrewd, vain, ambitious, hungry for a place in the world) against Henleigh Grandcourt, the aristocrat who wishes to marry her, apparently setting in motion the classic struggle between a woman and a man who are evenly matched: in this case both cold, smart, and determined. In the bargain, Gwendolen seems malicious: she taunts and manipulates the arrogant lord as if the exercise of sexual power in and of itself is a necessary plesure. But slowly, steadily—it takes Eliot 200 pages to get them married—we are moved deeper inside Gwendolen and we see that her behavior is meant to be off-putting. She is desperate to keep the action going, delay the moment of decision. We see that she is buying time. She dreads marriage. "It was not," Eliot observes of her, "that she wished to damage men, it was only that she wished not to be damaged by them."

Beneath the prettiness and the shrewd frivolity lies an astonishing maturity. Behind her young eyes Gwendolen is growing older by the minute. She thinks of her impending marriage, and she feels the steady pressure of her husband's will bearing down on her. Nothing, she knows, can avert that. Even if Grandcourt's courtship indicates real feeling, that he is actually in love with her and intends to deliver on his promises, she knows that her freedom is going—forever. The insight panics her. What to do, what to do. The question beats against her thoughts. Her mind becomes a cage. She cannot think. Her heart, already cold, hardens. Then her resistance collapses. She grows weary, so weary. One last time she cries out. All she wants is to be free! She would give *anything* to not marry, not marry at all. But of course Gwendolen would not give anything, she can't give anything, because Eliot cannot imagine her giving anything. All Eliot can do is justify her fears. She makes Grandcourt a monster who holds Gwendolen a prisoner inside her privileged life. Four years after the marriage Gwendolen stares into the endless future and wishes only for death—his or hers, it matters not which. She is twenty-two years old.

Edith Wharton's Lily Bart and Virginia Woolf's Clarissa Dalloway are variants of the woman who looks with clear sight on the life that follows the wedding, and goes cold at what she sees.

Lily Bart, like Gwendolen Harleth, is a woman divided against herself in a world of social rigidities that are not negotiable. Lily can neither face the decision to marry a bourgeois nor can she bear excommunication from the only world she knows. She keeps the action going longer than Gwendolen, sabotaging herself time after time until, finally, all that is left to her is a compromised marriage to an upstart Jew or suicide. She chooses suicide. Clarissa Dalloway, on the other hand, thinks she will save herself by refusing to marry the man she loves (as the force of his personality will, she knows, subsume her), taking instead a man so empty of will and emotion he does not object when she removes herself to a cold white sexlessness inside the marriage: another form of death-in-life.

Each of these three novels was written by a brilliant woman with the taste of iron in her mouth. Each of them gives us a sobering portrait of what it feels like to be the creature trapped, caught, stopped in place. Yet no one of these novels penetrates any deeper than the others into the character's desire to be free: all that is achieved here is the look and feel of resistance. But what exactly is it that is wanted? What is the struggle all about? Where is the line of inner division drawn, and of what is the capitulation composed? Some necessary distance on the subject is lacking. Or fullness of experience.

George Meredith, in his late fifties, had the experience and the distance. Meredith knew better than Woolf, Eliot, and Wharton what a woman and a man equally matched in brains, will, and hungriness of spirit might actually say and do, both to themselves and to one another. (Virginia Woolf thought him the most grown-up of Victorian novelists.) He knew how the conflicts would work themselves out: in him and in her. He understood *her* brilliantly. *Diana of the Crossways*—published in 1885—gives us a protagonist for whom love is the enemy the way Lawrence understood it to be the enemy, only this time we have the information from a woman in whom the need to own her soul is more imperative than the need to love. Meredith knew that a woman might better be driven than a man to the extremity of forgoing love. This was a piece of intelligence he possessed to a larger degree than almost any other writer of his time, and this is largely how he came by it.

In his early twenties Meredith married Mary Ellen Nicolls, the daughter of the poet Thomas Love Peacock. She was a widow six years older than he, a woman of independent opinion with a strong taste for the world. Sophisticated, passionate, as egotistical as he, she delighted and tormented him. They lived together for eight stormy years; then she had an affair and left him; when she repented and wanted to reconcile he stiffened in humiliated rage; three years later she was dead. Her name did not cross Meredith's lips for the rest of his long life, but he never forgot her. Or, rather, he never forgot himself with her. The memory of his own bad behavior haunted him, and what men and women could do to each other in love became his great preoccupation. In life Meredith was stubborn and angry but in his writing he acted on what he knew. In 1862 he wrote *Modern Love*, an astonishing poem based on his marriage to Mary Ellen. He wanted to trash her but he was a great poet; he could only stand back and see the situation whole. He saw that it was being locked into each other psycholgially that had made them both act so badly. Love, he concluded, was not a benign experience: not for him, and certainly not for her. Someday he would write a novel on the subject.

Diana Warwick is one of the first women in an English novel both beautiful and intellectually gifted who needn't be dismissed as vain, shrewd, and ambitious before we can get on with it. From the beginning, hers is the sympathetic point of view. When we meet her she is young, lovely, appealing in speech and manner, belonging by right of birth and expectation to the aristocracy but alone in the world with no money (very much like Lily Bart), in a position of need that only marriage can rectify. Marry she must, and marry she does.

Bold in the naivete of her good looks and high spirits, Diana takes the first presentable man who comes along, Mr. Warwick. The marriage is her education. She sees quickly that she has yoked herself for life to a man of narrow mind and pinched feeling whose company depresses and isolates her. At the same time she discovers that she is unwilling—no, *unable*—to accept her situation, settle down to it. She finds in herself a passion for political talk and, in London, develops friendships among those in public office; one especially with an MP old enough to be her father who values her conversation to an inordinate degree. Diana's husband feels the sting of her independence. He broods on it, then falls into a rage, brings suit against her, naming the MP as corespondent. But he cannot prove his case. The Warwicks separate and, with her reputation barely intact, Diana sets herself up as a political hostess and begins writing novels and articles to make a living. Soon her books are being reviewed, and every MP in town wants to have dinner at Diana's.

She blossoms into a glorious creature. Her mind grows tough, honest, wise, her speech witty, her insights luminous. She is unsentimental. She takes in her own experience. After the separation, alone for the first time, in "lodgings," Diana receives her friend Lady Emma, who is appalled, and asks if she can really like this. Diana replies, "I do. Yes, I can eat when I like, walk, work—and I am working! My legs and my pen demand it. Let me be independent! Besides, I begin to learn something of the bigger world outside the one I know, and I crush my mincing tastes. In return for that, I get a sense of strength I had not when I was a drawing room exotic. Much is repulsive. But I am taken with a passion for reality!"

The independence allows her to see herself as never before. In speaking of why her husband brought suit against her, she says, "He has not cause to like his wife. . . . We walked a dozen steps in stupefied union, and hit upon crossways. From that moment it was tug and tug; he me, I him. By resisting, I made him a tyrant; and he, by insisting, made me a rebel. . . . I despised him too much, and I showed it. He is not a contemptible man before the world; he is merely a very narrow one under close inspection. I could not—or did not—conceal my feelings. I showed it."

She becomes a gifted conversationalist. Meredith lets us see her through a long description of the talk at her dinner table. Diana is a creator of the talk not by virtue of a *saloniste*'s manipulation of her guests, but through her own high participation. The description is one only a man who needs good conversation could have written. Meredith loves Diana because she talks! He pays her the highest compliment by saying of her evenings, "They rose from the table at ten, with the satisfaction of knowing that they had not argued, had not wrangled, had never stagnated, and were digestingly refreshed; as it should be among grown members of the civilized world, who mean to practice philosophy, making the hour of the feast a balanced recreation and regeneration of body and mind."

As Diana's intelligence strengthens it takes in ever harder truths. She begins to see that her independence is intimately related to the clarity of her thought, and she comes to believe that the increasing goodness of her mind is linked to passions held in check. Passionate feeling, she is persuaded, is the undoing of a woman's independence. Diana gazes with a cold, clear eye—remarkably cold—at her calculation of life's cost. In London it is said of her that she is cold by nature. We, too, see her as cold, but not by nature.

Enter Percy Dacier, rising politico, and Diana's match in age, temperament, ambition: also cold, very cold, and for reasons that are similar to Diana's yet not equal in value. These two fall in love. From the beginning the emotion means something different to each of them. Percy is enchanted by Diana's brains ("She quickened a vein of imagination that gave him entrance to a strangely brilliant sphere, above his own, where, she sustaining, he too could soar"), but determined as well to arouse her senses ("He did not object to play second to her sprightly wits in converse, if he had some warm testimony to his mastery over her blood"). Diana, in turn, experiencing desire, feels all her stifled longing surface ("Had she beauty and rich health in the young summer blooming of her days—and all doomed to waste?"), then is quickly reminded of her tenuous position in the world.

Percy rises in Parliament and Mr. Warwick becomes desperately ill. With hope in the offing, their feelings begin to get the better of them. One night, after the others have left Diana's house, Percy doubles back to tell her a political secret that had been entrusted to him that very day. Diana becomes excited. The secret eroticizes them. Unexpectedly, he takes hold of her. She feels herself yielding. He betrays a sense of triumph: she is magnificent, but he must see her subdued. She pulls back instantly. Her passion struggles with her fear. Fear becomes hatred. She sends him away. Then, in one of the most extraordinary scenes ever written, she goes out into the street at midnght, takes a cab to the office of the most powerful newspaper editor in London, and leaks Percy's secret. Next morning—with the story in the paper—Percy comes to her. She confesses. He stares at her. "You sold me to a journalist." Her mouth opens and shuts without a sound. It is only now that she realizes what she has actually done. She has nothing to say. They part forever. The second most extraordinary scene ever written.

Why does Diana do it? Why does she betray the man she loves and dishonor herself? What has driven her to become an antisocial protagonist? a corrupted heroine? a stunningly not-nice girl? Whom does she fear, Percy or herself? Conquest from without, or subjugation from within? And why does it matter so much? What is really at stake?

The scene in which Diana rushes off to the newspaper office at midnight is the crucial one in the book. When we arrive at it we know it was inevitable, from the beginning, that the dazzling Diana herself would bring about the death of love. For her, no other course is possible. The scene is immensely complicated, its meaning still open to debate. Here's how I read it.

After Percy leaves her, Diana rushes about the room in a sudden fever, plunged in crisis, reviling herself. Who is she, what is she, she can't really write, doesn't really make money, has nothing of value, no one respects her, why should anyone respect her, she is only a woman alone, an actress, an adventuress, a poseur. Her head throbs. She is overcome by the memory of Percy's embrace:

> She pressed her hands on her eyelids. Would Percy have humiliated her so if he had respected her? . . . The lover's behavior was judged by her sensations: she felt humiliated. . . . Something that was pressing her low, she knew not how, and

left it unquestioned, incited her to exaggerate the indignity her pride had suffered. . . . She laid the scourge on her flesh smartly—I gave him these privileges because I am weak as the weakest, base as my enemies proclaim me. I covered my woman's vile weakness with an air of intellectual serenity that he, choosing his moment, tore away, exposing me to myself, as well as to him.

She casts wildly about for solace and solution. What is it she needs? What will give her comfort? Money, she answers herself. That's it. Money is what she needs. If she had money, *none* would dare take liberties. What has she got to sell? . . . Her writing she knows will never succeed . . . Percy's news! . . . After all, he didn't really say it was a secret. . . .

With that she calls her maid and begins to dress. The maid puts on her furs: "Not paid for! was Diana's desperate thought, and a wrong one. But she had to seem the precipitated bankrupt . . . and she succeeded."

Out in the street they hail a hansom. Inside the cab Diana keeps up a stready stream of words: "She talked her cool philosophy to mask her excitement from herself." Excitement is the key word.

In the newspaper office she waits while men rush back and forth, ignoring her presence. She is not really disturbed at being ignored. She is, in fact, more excited. One feels continuously her mounting excitement.

Then, suddenly, the dirty deed is done and the high is over.

Coming out of the editor's room, "She breathed deeply from time to time, as if under a weight, or relieved of it, but she seemed animated." Later at home she has tea, and then it is as though "Diana had stunned herself with the strange weight of the expedition, and had not a thought. In spite of the tea at that hour she slept soundly through the remainder of the night, dreamlessly til late into the morning"—when Percy comes to see her.

In this scene a writer of great intelligence lays out a no-win situation. His character is driven to perform an act that goes against every value she and her world hold in common. This she cannot do if she is fully conscious of what she is doing—as which of us could?—so what we have on the page is a Diana in a state of semiawareness, acting badly, as though in a dream, anesthetizing herself to commit a kind of self-mutilation that seems to her like necessary surgery.

It is not so much that Diana fears the imposition of Percy's will on her as that, in the moment she had felt herself falling toward him, she had known she would subjugate herself to love, and once lost to love, she is convinced, she will no longer be able to think—less and less will she have her thoughts, her own thoughts—and *that* is what she wants. She prizes the clarity of thought she has struggled so hard to gain: her independence is tied to it. She had also known—again in that same moment— that if Percy came after her she would not have the strength to hold out against him. So she decides to do something that will put her beyond the pale: that way the choice will be made for her. She'd rather place herself on the other side of the law (their law) than become a prisoner of her own weakest self. She will be vile but she will be free. Free to enter herself. Love, she knows, is not the way in. Into herself is through the mind, not through the senses. That is what freedom means to Diana.

She is wrong, of course. She will not be free. Free is not through the working mind or the gratified senses; free is through the steady application of self-understanding. Diana is too angry and too frightened to be free. In her panic she savages Percy and deforms herself. Like an animal in a frenzy, she tears loose of the trap, leaving behind a limb. For the rest of her life she will lick a wound covered over by scar tissue. Courage she has in great measure; it is self-knowledge she lacks.

All that fear and anger is the alarming reality that *Diana of the Crossways* so abundantly lays out. Love, Meredith wants us to know, is a deadly busines: it throws us up against ourselves and leaves us hanging there. No one who engages seriously in it emerges without a sense of having been violated and, most often, of having committed the violation oneself. In a curious way, Meredith is saying, love is not to the point at all: the antagonism one feels within oneself in its presence is far more crucial. Once *that* is made clear to a writer (and by a writer), love as an end in itself begins to lose influence.

Meredith is to Diana as Flaubert is to Emma Bovary: she is himself. By making Diana the brilliant creature she is, and letting her live fully inside the life of an intelligent woman who

craves independence — that is, by making the situation *acute* —
Meredith was better able to get at those elements that unleash
the mortified and unknowing self: his real interest, his own
wound. Diana is brave and decent, but when gripped by her
fears and driven by her hungers, she acts like a cornered animal. With all her intelligence and high-mindedness she cannot
bring her stricken emotions under control. She is doomed to act
badly. This, Meredith knew, was the deeper truth about human relations.

As the twentieth century has progressed, Meredith's sense of
things has grown steadily. What was once a footnote to a doctrine
begins to seem like the text itself. A preoccupation with the
frightened, angry self dominates the culture, and the need to
clarify — to purge the strickenness at the center — has become a
commonplace in our system of imperatives. That need chal-
lenges successfully the longing to be swept away.

Meredith's great forgotten novel brings these thoughts into fo-
cus. The language is of another century as is the social circumstance, but the central interest in Diana's headlong plunge toward herself is of a remarkable immediacy. When Diana's love
affair goes on the rocks, we are not at all awash in regret, so ab-
sorbing are the *real* events of her inner life — the excitement of
her false independence, the swiftness with which she spins out
of control, the ugliness when she feels threatened — and so moving the intelligence with which she tries to take in the meaning
of what she has lived. It is the drama of the self we are wit-

nessing—that astonishing effort to climb up out of original shame—and the awful, implicit knowledge that love, contrary to all sentimental insistence, cannot do the job for us. For better and for worse, that effort is a solitary one, more akin to the act of making art than of making family. It acknowledges, even courts, loneliness. Love, on the other hand, fears loneliness, turns sharply away from it.

A great metaphor reflects that portion of the shared experience which promises self-understanding. That we would know ourselves—or see that we *couldn't* know ourselves, or didn't *want* to know ourselves—was once the promise of Nature in literature; then of God; then of Love. For the time being, at least, Love seems to have gone the way of Nature and of God. We are cast adrift, radically "alone" now, in literature as in life, groping in the books we write to find the metaphoric elements that will achieve new power. If you would feel persuaded that "the time being" has been in the works for a hundred years, read *Diana of the Crossways*.

Clover Adams

]⁓[

ON THE EVE of her engagement to Henry Adams in February of 1872, Clover Hooper wrote a letter to her sister, Ellen, recounting a dream in which the two of them had been sitting side by side, with a wall of ice between them; when Ellen married, the ice on her side of the wall melted, but Clover's ice remained in the shade, unable to thaw. For a long time, she said, her waking life had resembled that dream but now, she went on, a strong sun had begun to shine, and "the ice has all melted away." Henry, too, had looked forward to coming in out of the cold; just before the wedding he'd written a friend that he thought them a perfectly matched pair, and that they were "sure to paddle along through life with all the fine weather and sunshine there is in it." That was in the spring. In June they married. Thirteen years later, in December of 1885, in the middle of one of the most companionate marriages on record, Clover Adams drank a bottle of cyanide and died. The ice had formed itself around her again, thicker than ever, this time encasing her completely.

Henry was stunned. He had thought them integral parts of one another—two halves of a single whole, like characters in a story—and he had assumed she felt the same. Her suicide was not only an abandonment but a message to the world that all this time she had been a creature apart; in possession of a secret self; a quantity unknown and, in the end, unknowable.

They *were* something like characters in one of the large novels of their century. But whose? Who would have written them? Hardy? Gissing? Eliot? Not Hardy; in Hardy they'd have been passionate, brooding creatures, flinging themselves headlong into their awful destinies. Gissing wouldn't have gotten them right either; in him fastidiousness would have turned out priggish. Eliot. She would have understood them perfectly—high-minded, thin-skinned, full of wounded self-regard—and she would have given them both their due, especially Clover. I think George Eliot would have imagined Clover Adams fully.

⤚

She was born in Boston in 1843 to Ellen Sturgis and William Hooper, children of the established merchant class, rich, connected, and somewhat intellectual. When they met, William was a young doctor and Ellen one of the women in Margaret Fuller's conversation circle. The marriage was loving and no doubt would have continued on peacefully, but Ellen was tubercular and died at thirty-six, leaving William with three young children. A remarkably tender man who never married again, the doctor lavished all his love and attention on the children; especially on four-year-old Clover who'd been a soul mate from her nearly motherless beginning.

Henry Adams, grandson and great-grandson of presidents, grew up famously self-doubting in a family awash in nervous disorder: cold and withholding, emotionally eccentric (the worst review of Henry's first book was written anonymously in *The Nation* by his older brother Charles). Henry sometimes joked that he was lucky to have been born the fourth child in a large brood—that way he'd been overlooked and left happily alone—but this joke, like all other Henry Adams jokes, had the taste of ashes in it. There was in him, from the beginning, a bitter forlornness that deprived him of self-belief. He might just as well have been motherless.

When Clover's sweet-tempered sister, Ellen, and the unworldly Harvard dean, Whitman Gurney, became husband and wife, they fell, unexpectedly, into a marital bliss that astonished everyone who knew them—a Hooper aunt said Ellen's nakedly happy face on the streets of Cambridge should be veiled—but those at Harvard ambitious for the world were somewhat patronizing in their congratulations: among these Henry Adams, and perhaps secretly even Clover herself. Clover had not grown up sweet, she had grown up smart; more than smart; sharp-tongued and intellectually mocking. When Henry got his first real taste of her Austen-like conversation he was beside himself with gratitude. Her humor was as black as his own. He couldn't believe his luck. He, like she, had thought the loneliness would never end; that he'd never make connection; and now, here he had a soul mate, a twin.

The ground they met on was this: the defensive posture of each had become stylish scorn. Both took excessive delight in caustic wit, derisive criticality, and intellectual outrage. They could, neither of them, simply like a thing or not. They were people for whom judgment and corrective are a moral necessity. This habit of mind became an imperative that shaped the approach to inner life. It would, inevitably, have had to include a discriminating assessment of each other. But only his got committed to paper.

Henry's letters about Clover on the eve of his marriage are famous and have often been quoted to demonstrate his misogyny, but to me they read like the words of a man who, embarrassed by his own feeling and fearing the judgment he himself so readily dispenses, "admits" to everything before he can be "accused" of it. So, on the one hand, he writes to his brother, Brooke, "On coming to know Clover Hooper, I found her so far away superior to any woman I had ever met, that I did not think it worthwhile to resist," but he then quickly confides of his future bride that she is "certainly not handsome . . . talks garrulously, but on the whole pretty sensibly . . . is very open to instruction . . . dresses badly . . . decidedly has humor and will appreciate *our* wit." Later, writing in the same vein, he tells a friend that "my young female has a very active and quick mind and has run over many things, but she really knows nothing well, and laughs at the idea of being thought a blue." Then, ever qualifying, he says, "I think you will like her, not for beauty, for she is certainly not beautiful, and her features are much too prominent; but for intelligence and sympathy, which are what hold me."

Henry *knows* that self-doubt is making him disloyal to the richness of feeling Clover has brought into his life; at the end of one of these letters he writes the conventionally humorous sentence, "She rules me as only American women rule men, and I cower before her," then quickly cries out, "Lord! how she would lash me if she read the above description of her!" Yet, judgment and corrective never stopped. On the day of their engagement Henry all but announced, "These are the terms, never in future say I didn't warn you" by giving Clover a copy of the new William Dean Howells novel, *The Wedding Journey*. It's difficult not to wonder what he *thought* he was doing.

The setting of this novel is a honeymoon trip to Niagara Falls. The protagonist, Basil March, is enamored of his new wife, Isabel; yet he thinks her ignorant ("His wife, as a true American woman, knew nothing of the history of her country"), and that her sexual hold on him makes him bow to what he sees as the natural pettiness of a woman's character (Isabel provokes a quarrel and then compels Basil to give in; when he does, she meets "his surrender with the openness of a heart that forgives but does not forget"). One day the couple walks out across a series of small bridges hanging over the falls and, suddenly, Isabel experiences a terror she cannot bring under control. Unnerved by the torrential floods of water, she sinks down, declaring that she cannot walk back. Howells writes that Basil "stared at her cowering form in blank amaze." At last, she recovers and walks ashore, but thereafter Basil "treated Isabel . . . with a superiority which he felt himself to be very odious, but which he could not disuse." The novel is remarkably open in its depiction of the power struggle alive beneath the calm wedded surafce. Once married, judgment was something one would be living intimately with: for weeks and months and years.

The day after the wedding Clover wrote the first of the weekly Sunday letters she would send her father from Washington and Europe during the thirteen years of her marriage. Addressed "Dear Pater," these very well written letters, brimming with life, are a running account of her daily doings. When writing from Europe, there is travel and society to describe. She hates the British (as Henry James wearily attested) and never tires of trashing them:

> The hour after dinner, with two stupid Englishwomen, was rather severe, though as a study of character it was amusing. . . . In the huge ballroom some large Sir Joshuas did their best to atone for the present owner's vile taste. . . . For sordid niggardliness no one can beat a Britisher. They save on table linen, towels, candles and fires, flowers and underclothes, to put monkey-jackets on their servants. . . . England

is charming for a new families but hopeless for most. . . . Thank the lord that the American eagle flaps and screams over us.

When writing from home, politics replaces social observation. "Sunday, a pleasant dinner—Carl Schurz, Aristarchi Bey (a Turkish diplomat) and Mr. Belmont, and Mr. Nordhoff after dinner—all politics and public affairs" begins one of innumerable letters (this one written in April of 1882) that include gossip and commentary on the gross failings of nearly everyone in Washington. But in the main, the letters are long descriptions of dinner parties given and attended, houses rented and furnished, paintings and watercolors considered and bought. Up until the very end, they include lists of guests; descriptions of flowering trees and bushes seen from the window (japonica, magnolia, and forsythia); accounts of the ongoing construction of their new house; and always the consideration of some object of beauty with an eye to buying (all her life Clover was a passionate consumer of beautiful and tasteful things, her house as much a place of elegance as of social discrimination). A month before Dr. Hooper dies, on a trip to New York she visits a gallery and writes,

> I saw there a superb old Chinese dish, jade color—tracery under the dull glaze—about two feet in diameter and turned up at right angles, a brim about three inches, deliciously modelled, made beyond everything for five lily pads and four

white lilies—one hundred and seventy five dollars. I don't wish to put so much money in anything so easily broken, but it is hauntingly fascinating.

This letter is heartbreaking for the pleasure it takes in the things of the world, its delight in description, its fineness of interest and detachment, and the fact that it is written only months before she killed herself.

Clover's letters to her father are uniformly calm, intelligent, and observant and somehow in them, she seems delighted to be in the world. It's not that she doesn't have some hard, mocking things to say about the people around her, of course she does—she wouldn't know who she is if she wasn't exercising the critical faculty—but in some indefinable way the overriding interest in judgment feels suspended here. The writing is endowed with equanimity. The relief of simple appreciation is everywhere apparent. In her father's conjured presence some necessary distance—the one needed to let imagination run free, the one Henry achieved through his work—is suddenly hers. The act of writing to her father seems to open her to herself—make her able to "speak" with herself—in a way, perhaps, that she could with him but not with her husband.

Between them, Henry and Clover knew "everyone." Through their letters (his and hers) troop Lowells and Jameses and Peabodys: as well as Holmes, Emerson, and Agassiz. Later on, in England and then in Washington, it would be diplomats and historians, writers and architects, politicians and aristocrats, and every American president from Lincoln to Roosevelt. Together, the life they made was one of books and travel and relentless socializing. "Much good talk at dinner" is a phrase that runs steadily through years of letter writing—and the dinner was usually eaten at their table.

Clover Adams was perhaps Washington's first great *saloniste*. Henry had the name and the connections but it was Clover— with a talent for conversation equal if not superior to Henry's— who created the atmosphere of intellectual grace that made their home on Lafayette Square a major gathering place for more than a decade. An invitation to five o'clock tea at the Adamses was much sought after: which led to triumph for those who got it and anguish for those who did not. In time, of course, most did not—"the complaint was made [of the house]," Henry James wrote, "that it was too limited, that it left out, on the whole, more people than it took in"—and the enterprise turned in on itself. For a while, though, five o'clock tea at the Adamses achieved an ideal of true society—a dailiness of shared mind and spirit—significant enough to influence the thought and feeling of those who were in on it for years to come, especially the small group known as the Five of Hearts.

One afternoon in December of 1880 the writer and diplomat John Hay, who'd known Henry at Harvard, came to tea bringing along with him his good friend, Clarence King, the brilliant and famous geologist who'd mapped the fortieth parallel (thus opening the West for the railroads) and was now head of the first U.S. Geological Survey. These two, in conversation with Clover and Henry, struck a spark, delighting to an unusual degree in the sentences that came pouring out of their own mouths in each other's company. The pleasure was so strong that the conversation passed from tea to dinner and then on until midnight. The next day the exercise was repeated. They continued to meet (Hay soon brought his wife, Clara, along as well) day after day, and so bonded that they began to call themselves the Five of Hearts. In March of 1881 a new presidential administration dispensed with the services of Hay and King, and both men temporarily decamped from Washington. They were to meet, and keep track of one another, as long as they lived (they even wrote to each other on Five of Hearts stationery), but never again would they achieve the dailiness of those few magical months that lived on in memory, for all of them, as their lost Eden.

Together, these people were an incarnation of the American democracy: the Boston Brahmin, the intellectual man-of-action, the politically skilled westerner. They were all (except for Clara Hay) immensely intelligent, immensely gifted, and immensely depressed. John Hay (who began as personal secretary to Lincoln and ended as secretary of state to Theodore Roosevelt) hated his life as a diplomat, and every afternoon—everywhere in the world—fell into despair. Clarence King, longing for domestic tranquillity but unable to make connection with a woman of his own class, drove himself from one failed project to another, slowly losing touch with everyone who mattered to him, dying destitute and alone in the West; after his death it was discovered he'd had a black common-law wife and five children in Brooklyn with whom he lived from time to time under an assumed name. The gloom of Henry Adams—the form it took, the years it lasted, the conclusion it made him reach—is well known. And Clover, afflicted with the malady of the age, was repeatedly plunged into a case of "nerves."

All these men—a diplomat, a historian, a paid wanderer—struggled mightily with demons they could not master. But every day, throughout their lives, each one went out to do battle with the world; doing battle with the world allowed them to do battle with themselves; doing battle with themselves they brought their miseries under enough control to achieve sufficient detachment; achieving detachment they did the work that gives human existence its meaning.

Henry Adams worked each day as a historian, a journalist, a political mentor and intriguer: depressed but active: depressed but influential: depressed but taking himself seriously. The vituperation of Henry's self-loathing did not yield as the years went on—in the late 1880s Clarence King said, "I am a comic opera beside Henry Adams whose grim gray scorn of this universe seems to me very ashen and disembodied"—but the mind prevailed. He did what was expected of him, and in the end it saved him.

Clover had no similar relief: nothing was expected of her. She ran the salon, she socialized skillfully, she exercised a wit that as time passed yielded less pleasure, less energy, less meaning. In short: she had no work. No work meant inner drift. The men in her circle were each compelled by inner necessity to convert disability to virtue—especially Henry whose genius it was to make of his own self-doubt an instrument of historic interpretation— but Clover remained an intelligent woman who feared being thought a blue, condemned to back off from the only kind of struggle that would have sufficiently freed her from the same conviction of inner worthlessness that dogged the men around her. With no useful way to vent themselves, her anxieties went underground where they increasingly transformed into postures of spiritual inertness, hesitating thought, demoralized will. In time she became that which women were accused of being by nature.

Henry understood that Clover's passivity was really his own: he knew inner drift intimately. He saw himself in her. He'd always seen himself in her. Not a good or a hopeful or an encouraging self, but rather the unnerved and endlessly appraising self, the one that gave back judgment. Not steadily, of course; if it had been steady they would have been unhappy together. The atmosphere between them remained fluid—antagonisms were low-grade, reconciliations understated—but it was marked by conflicts that repeatedly broke through the unconscious, revealing a divided state of emotional affairs.

Mabel Hooper (Clover's niece), in a memoir of her famous

aunt and uncle, remembered them in the early 1870s: "Often in the afternoon, the nieces would watch—almost enviously—the two figures on horseback vanishing into the flickering sunlight of the woods. An impression of oneness of life and mind, of perfect companionship, left an ideal never to be effaced." But during this very same period Henry was writing in a much-quoted letter:

> My wife ... studies Greek. All our young women study Greek. It has become the correct thing to do. ... [They] are haunted by the idea that they ought to read, or labor in some way, not for any such frivolous object as making themselves agreeable to society, nor for simple amusement, but "to improve their minds." They are utterly unconscious of the pathetic impossibility of improving those hard, thin, one-stringed instruments which they call their minds, and which haven't range enough to master one big emotion, much less to express it in words or figures.

It was self-contempt that made Henry write that letter. The same self-contempt that made him scornful of the world made him identify, disastrously, with his wife. He never hated himself more than when he was deriding Clover; that, indeed, is where "two became as one." The thesis is laid out like a map of the psychological terrain in the two novels Henry wrote, *Democracy* and *Esther*. In each of them he creates a female protagonist modeled on Clover but endowed with anxieties, hungers, and half-hidden motives that are undeniably his own. The negative feeling applied to this double creation is startling.

"For reasons which many persons thought ridiculous," begins *Democracy*, "Mrs. Lightfoot Lee decided to pass the winter in Washington. . . . It was only to her closest intimates that she honestly acknowledged herself to be tortured by *ennui*."

Madeleine Lee is Henry's Candide. Ambitious to discover the meaning of life, she has tried society, she has tried philosophy, she has tried virtue; all have failed her; now she intends to try power. She must try *some*thing: her ennui has had consequences. Compelled to complain at New York dinner parties of the pigmylike stature of human endeavor — "You grow six inches high, and then you stop. Why will not somebody grow to be a tree and cast a shadow?" — Madeleine Lee has outstayed her welcome in the city. "'What does the woman want?' New York society was asking. 'What need is there for abusing us just because she feels herself no taller than we are? What does she expect to get from her sharp tongue? What does she know, anyway?'" Indeed, the omniscient author agrees, and confides in the reader that "Mrs. Lee certainly knew very little. She had read voraciously and promiscuously one subject after another," but although "Ruskin and Taine had danced merrily through her mind, hand in hand with Darwin and Stuart Mill, Gustave Droz and Algernon Swinburne," she had actually made little sense of what she read ("Though not brighter than her neighbors, the world persisted in classing her among clever women"). Now, however, we are told, she has been fired with a visionary quest:

She wanted to see with her own eyes the action of primary forces; to touch with her own hand the massive machinery of society; to measure with her own mind the capacity of the motive power. She was bent upon getting to the heart of the great American mystery of democracy and government. . . . What she wished to see, she thought, was the clash of interests, the interests of forty millions of people and a whole continent, centering at Washington; guided, restrained, controlled, or unrestrained and uncontrollable, by men of ordinary mould; the tremendous forces of government, and the machinery of society, at work. What she wanted was POWER.

This portrait of Mrs. Lightfoot Lee is a perfect mixture of Clover's shortcomings as Henry sees them, and his own half-acknowledged drives. Yes, Clover was restless and ambitious; yes, she did not make sufficient sense of what she read; yes, she was openly scornful at dinner parties. But it was himself, not her, who was obsessed with getting close to POWER, and whose only excuse for doing so was wanting to touch "the heart of the great American mystery."

In *Esther*, the situation centers not on politics, but on the struggle between reason and religion. Esther Dudley is an amateur painter who lives in New York with her adored, freethinking father. While she is helping to decorate the interior of a newly constructed cathedral, its appealing minister, Stephen Hazard, falls in love with her. After her father dies, Esther thinks she too is in love, and accepts Hazard's proposal of marriage. During the engagement period she nearly loses her wits, trying to square her relentlessly secular spirit with the prospect of becoming a minister's wife. She can't do it, and the novel ends with Esther breaking the engagement.

Once again, Henry endows his protagonist with much of Clover as he has continued over all the years of their marriage to see her: Esther has "a bad figure, imperfect features, no very good points . . . the instinct of power, but not the love of responsibility . . . is only a second-rate amateur and will never be anything more . . . picks up all she knows without an effort and knows nothing well . . . [has a] mind as irregular as her face." True, she is interesting—"She has a style of her own. . . . She gives one the idea of a lightly sparred yacht in mid-ocean; unexpected; you ask yourself what the devil she is doing there"—but her interestingness does not weight in the balance.

It's hard to believe in Esther's attachment to Hazard. The contest of wills between them feels spurious, instrumental to the plot. We can, however, readily see her relation to the omniscient author: *they* know one another well. At the book's conclusion Esther is left deflated—alone with the emptiness and the "absence" with which she began—and so is her creator. There is no question but that he shares her destiny. Neither of them is any closer at the end to inner clarity than at the beginning.

What is most striking about *Democracy* is the enormity of its emotional distance. It's not so much that the characters are held in contempt—the mockery is actually spread thin—as that the sympathy necessary to make characters real is entirely absent. The irony, levelled at one and all, is unremitting. It alone prevails. No other note is struck in the prose, no other view of things can be taken. *Esther*, on the other hand, is awash in depression.

When Henry wrote *Democracy* in 1880 he was restless; three years later when he wrote *Esther* he was probably in a rage. He was forty-six years old, and he was as he had always been. Within himself, he remained unchanged. Marriage had not made the vital difference.

What was Clover feeling? We do not know. We can never know. It is a characteristic of "lesser lives" that they leave behind nothing of the rich documentation of the lives with which they are associated, that which leads historians into plausible deduction. With lesser lives we are simply told "the sister was neurasthenic, the bride bolted, the wife was a suicide"—and there we are, alone with the shocking and dramatic conclusion. All we can do is speculate.

Certainly, she had read *Esther*, but what had she made of it? Nowhere, in any of her letters, does she say. We know only that now, in the winter of 1883, she had become dangerously bored. Everything and everyone was tiresome to her. Besieged by arrivistes, she had come to hate her own five o'clocks. ("Life is like a prolonged circus here now," she wrote her father.) People still came to dinner, but she no longer cared to go out. Ladies' luncheons were "a style of killing time which I detest"; diplomatic dinners were attended by people with brains "attenuated to a startling degree"; large parties were "hot rooms and crowds" that "take so much more from one than they give." She preferred to stay home and read.

How could it have been otherwise? In any life, the doubts, the depressions, the absence of self-belief—if not engaged with—progressively worsen, moving ineluctably from occasional ailment to recurrent episode to chronic condition. The condition occupies space, eats up air, consumes energy. Energy that should have fed experience now feeds the unlived life. The unlived life is not a quiescent beast. The unlived life is a little animal in a great rage, barely permitting of survival. And sometimes not even that. Sometimes, it ends an assassin.

In 1884 Henry wrote John Hay that he and Clover were "becoming green with mould. We are bored to death with ourselves, and see no one else. At long intervals we chirp feebly to each other, then sleep and dream sad dreams." Clover herself allowed, in a letter to a friend, that they were not as happy as before. The company they had always provided one another now began to confer loneliness rather than dissipate it. Henry locked himself in his study to work. Clover read, and looked out the window; read, and gazed into the fire; read, and wandered around the house. What was she thinking about during those bitter afternoons in the winter of 1885? What did she make of her life—of what she had done with it, and not done with it? How could she imagine things changing? Where was the change to come from? Henry had his work: out of work came, always, the hope of regeneration. What did she have? She had only their clever, mocking exchange, the one that year by year was sounding ever more hollow in her ears, the words often leaving her with an ashen taste in the mouth. True, she did have her Sunday letter to her father, *that* made her feel like a human being.

In March, Clover's father was stricken with angina. She went to Cambridge to help nurse him, and remained there until April when he died. Henry stayed on in Washington, writing daily to her. Much has been made of these letters, of the embarrassed re-move in them. "Madam," begins the first, "As it is now thirteen years since my last letter to you, you may have forgotten my name. If so, try to recall it. For a time we were somewhat inti-mate" . . . and ends, "There remains at the bottom of the page just a little crumb of love for you, but you must not eat it all at once. The dogs need so much." She knew what he *meant* to say, of course, and she well understood how hard it was for him to say it. In his place she would probably have been writing the same letter. Therein lay the prison-of-self they had constructed for themselves in their life together.

While her father was dying Clover was cheerful, steady, and brave. Afterward, she realized what had happened and went into free fall. A vital lifeline had been cut. She could not catch hold, could not right herself, pull out of her spin. She cried out once for help— "Ellen I'm not real—oh make me real—You are all of you real," she wrote to her sister—but she was spiraling down fast. Self-revilement—always there just beneath the withering wit—yanked her even harder. "If I had one single point of character or goodness I would stand on that and grow back to life," she wrote—and hit the ground.

She began staring into space. She'd be sitting, talking with people, and she'd break off in the middle of a sentence, rubbing her forehead, as though trying to remember where she was and what it was she'd been doing. Then she'd simply fall silent— she'd forgotten the people in the room—and sit staring.

Henry was beside himself. "[He] is more patient and loving than words can express," she wrote. "God might envy him—he bears and hopes and despairs hour after hour . . . the soul of kindness, sweet and attentive." By now she must have hated him. He meant well, but meaning well was no longer to the point. After all, what could *he* do for her that she could not do for herself? He was her brother, her soul mate, her twin. She looked at him, and saw her own worst view of herself coming back at her. What did he know that she did not? What he was in his own unchanged self—what they were *together*—that, apparently, was what now mattered. On her honeymoon trip she had included in a letter to her father a funny drawing meant to show herself and Henry laid low by seasickness, but it looks as though they are lying side by side in their coffins. In a way, perhaps, she had been buried with him. The years they had spent holding the world in clever contempt.

She killed herself on a Sunday afternoon in early December. They rose late, as usual, and had breakfast at noon. I can just see them, Henry probably reading the paper aloud to her, thinking to take her mind off the letter she usually wrote on Sunday. Listen to this, he might have said in his amused, cutting voice, and then there would have been fourteen negatives in six sentences. She must have rubbed her forehead and stared into space as he spoke. The casual, predictable scorn in his voice. . . . It was her own voice coming back at her. . . . She could hear that. . . . The voice in which she'd spoken all these years except when she was writing to her father. Now her father was dead. She looked up at Henry. She was alone with the scorn. She would always be alone with it. She stared into the future. She was forty-two years old. The ice formed itself around her, thick and numbing. Nothing could burn through that numbness, certainly not pain. She went upstairs and swallowed cyanide.

Kate Chopin

KATE CHOPIN BEGAN WRITING in 1888. She was thirty-eight years old, the widow of a New Orleans cotton factor. The stuff poured out of her: swift, sure, immediate, without hesitation and without revision. Very quickly, there was a novel, and a collection of stories. She published the novel (*At Fault*) herself but the book was favorably reviewed, and the stories (*Bayou Folk*) made their own way easily. In no time at all she was established. Her stories were set among the Creoles and Cajuns of rural Louisiana, and she was welcomed into American literature as a delightful regionalist whose work was wonderfully mimetic.

For more than a decade Chopin worked on as a popular, well-known writer. Then, in 1899, she published *The Awakening*. This novel came as a shock and a scandal. It was *not* delightful. It was realistic in the European style. More Zola than Zola, it was said. Too strong for the children, it was said. Should be labeled moral poison, it was said. Chopin was stunned. Why was this book being received so differently from her other work? After all, there was nothing here that she hadn't said, one way or another, before. It was all there in the stories. Surely people had seen that, hadn't they? No, it was explained, they hadn't. The stories had only implied what she was now saying openly.

Depression set in. She stopped writing. No doubt, given time, she would have come out the other side, but as it happened there was no time. In 1904 Kate Chopin suffered a brain hemmorhage and died. She was fifty-four years old. She left behind three novels, eighty-five stories, and a reputation as an "odd one" in American letters.

During her marriage Chopin had discovered that the strain of sensuality in herself was serious and the power of erotic love immense. It was a piece of understanding that became integrated into her inner life, and her stories were marked from the beginning by a startling adultness about sexual love. Two things in her work made this adultness palatable to American readers in the 1890s: the sex was among Creoles and Cajuns (for which read people not like ourselves), and it was never made explicit.

She had discovered something else as well: that under the best of circumstances marriage was an opposition of wills. One or the other of the married couple was always being gently, subtly, lovingly pushed out of shape; dominated; made to do the bidding of the other. Usually—but this was not her theme—it was the woman because it was the woman who came to married life the least experienced, untried and unknowing.

Women, more often than men, awakened from the long dream of adolescence to find themselves bound in perpetuity into their lives without any realization of how they had gotten there. Men suffered, too, from the condition—she could see that—but when all was said and done, after the awakening men knew better how to make use of the baptism by fire. Women were left staring into the fire.

A woman's life, she saw, was a metaphor for the consequence of this dream of life gone on too long. Knowledge, when it came, was often without the power to activate the chronically dormant will. Without action of the will, a vacuum formed. Into the vacuum flowed the force of domination. Men did not have to learn (or even understand) the imperative of the active will; they were born to it. Women, however, once they were made conscious, often remained frozen, impaled on Hamlet's conflict.

It was by far the more important of the two pieces of knowledge that Kate Chopin had gained in her marriage to her entirely amiable husband. By comparison, sensuality was child's play. But this, the matter of the inactive will, was elusive and shadowy; difficult to get hold of, even more difficult to hold onto. To show in a piece of writing how it worked, and to what it might lead, that indeed would be a worthy task. Two other American writers were struggling with similar perceptions at just around the same time: Henry James (in *Portrait of a Lady*) and Edith

Wharton (in *House of Mirth*). Chopin could not tackle the problem head-on until *The Awakening*.

The story is simplicity itself. Edna Pontellier, twenty-eight years old and the mother of two little boys, is married to Léonce, a Creole stockbroker. They are summering at Grand Isle, a beach resort that is to New Orleans as Fire Island is to New York. Here we will meet Adèle Ratignolle, lush, bovine, a devoted wife and mother; Mademoiselle Reisz, tiny, deformed, unmarried, an artist at the piano; Robert Lebrun, the hotelkeeper's son who flirts each summer with one married woman (this year, it's Edna). In the course of the summer Edna awakens sensually; she learns to swim, becomes alive to her own body, conceives a passion for Robert, discovers she has no interest — whatever — in being a wife or a mother. The young Robert returns her feeling. Frightened, he leaves for Mexico. The Pontelliers return to New Orleans where Edna drifts into a trance that deepens day by day. She stops caring for the house, wanders about the city, no longer responds to her husband's demands, visits Mademoiselle Reisz frequently. In this mood she takes up with unsavory people, allows herself to be seduced by a rake, and moves out of her husband's house. Then Robert returns from Mexico. She realizes that the affair was only a flirtation; he does not want her as she is and, worse, she does not want him. Throughout a long night Edna tries to make sense of her life, to understand what she has learned and what is before her. She cannot. She finds herself staring into the void. In the morning she takes the ferry to Grand Isle and walks into the sea.

The plot is melodrama, but the writing is powerful. Edna sees with eyes stripped of sentiment, and in language stripped of euphemism, exactly how things are with her. In passage after passage, she follows her thought to the logic of its own conclusion with breathtaking economy, making no detours and never falling short of arrival. The novel reads like a primer on the meaning and consequence of the (in)active will.

Yet the power of these many fine passages is not deeply woven into the inner structure of the novel. The clarity comes and goes until finally it just goes. Even devoted readers of *The Awakening* are made uneasy by the murkiness of the prose as the book nears its climax. I have read those pages describing Edna's dark night of the soul many times, and I still don't really know why she killed herself.

Nevertheless, the book has held me (so striking are the insights and the writing) as it has thousands of others, and I took to interpreting selectively to account for what makes me uncomfortable. At first I thought, She becomes sexual so she has to die. Then I thought, She looks into the pit, sees down to some essential emptiness of life, that's why she wants to die. Now I've read it again, and for the first time I see how fantasy-ridden Edna is. Her efforts at a life are rudimentary. (She has seen the light. Isn't that *enough*? Why aren't things falling into place? Why is it all still so *difficult*?) The pianist keeps telling her that art (self-creation) is never-ending hard work, but Edna cannot pay attention to what she is saying. Every little thing tires her out: immediately. She is forever sinking, exhausted, into Mademoiselle

Reisz's chair, or tottering through the streets, or ready to faint after a dinner party: a character in a Joan Didion novel. For a moment, now and then, she seems to understand what is required of her, grasp her anesthetized condition, but the moment passes and we see that she does not. More importantly, Kate Chopin does not.

Edith Wharton's Lily Bart and Henry James's Isabel Archer are both models for what ails Edna Pontellier. These characters are strongly American: modern creatures, divided against themselves. They say they want a real life, but they do not mean what they say. They do not understand that to have a life one must act, consciously and deliberately, on one's own integrated behalf. Neither Isabel nor Lily can do it; what's more, neither is prepared to accept the consequence for the failure to integrate.

Wharton and James both knew down to the ground this crucial thing about their characters—that they were paralyzed by self-division—and they created novels of penetrating intelligence because each writer knew well what the character knew only imperfectly. Kate Chopin knew only as much as Edna knew: not nearly enough. That is why her stories are only flashes of insight (strong but slight), and why the prose in *The Awakening* grows muddy and abstract.

Reading Chopin today I am struck anew by the extraordinary directness of the writing. Insight is simply thrown down on the page, bold, clear, even violent. The syntax is sophisticated but the directness is primitive: it occupies both foreground and background. Chopin sees a hard truth about what Willa Cather called the "inviolate self," and she views it from the perspective of a sexually adult woman. But she fails to place what she sees in a fully imagined world. This failure short-circuits the writer's intelligence, doesn't provide the room necessary to bring insight to wisdom.

One of her biographers makes the point that Chopin never revised. Chopin herself, announced, in interview after interview throughout her professional life, that the writing either came all at once, or not at all. I think it the single most important piece of information we have about her. She seems to have considered this startling practice a proof of giftedness, rather than of the amateurishness that it really was. After all, is a writer's life not *all* revision, nothing but revision? How else does thought clarify, and work deepen? How else move from insight to wisdom? See all around a thing, then down to the center? Create a world in a book, not just a glimpse through a open window?

She never got past the beginning. In her life and in her work it was all awakenings. But her preoccupations were those of two of the great writers of her time, and to a remarkable degree she made them hers as well.

Jean Rhys

THE COLLECTED LETTERS of Jean Rhys is one of those remarkable documents common in the lives of writers—a record of experience that both traces the writer's obsession to its biographical source and substantiates the claim, "I made it all up." Reading Rhys's letters it is easy to see how the striking early novels as well as the final brilliant one originate in and depart from what "really" happened. The letters are the life, and the novels—there's no mistaking it—are the magic performed on the life.

Rhys was born in the West Indies in 1894 to a Welsh father and a white Creole mother. She went to England at sixteen, spent two years at a school for girls in Cambridge, another at the Royal Academy of Dramatic Art in London, joined a touring company as a chorus girl, had a traumatic love affair with an older man who left her, married a semivagrant Dutch poet, wandered about Europe, met Ford Madox Ford in Paris, and began to write. Between 1927 and 1938 she published four novels that brought her a transitory bit of fame and no money at all. In 1938 she disappeared from London. Her books went out of print, and she was neither seen nor heard from again. In 1958 the BBC dramatized one of her novels (*Good Morning, Midnight*), and after twenty years of obscurity she was found living marginally in the English countryside with her third husband. Befriended by a pair of London book editors, Rhys was newly encouraged to write and, despite the extraordinary disorder of her daily life, she pulled out a manuscript that she had been working on for some years and began again. Published in 1966, *Wide Sargasso Sea* brought genuine fame and fortune. Her books were reprinted, and when she died in 1979 she was a literary celebrity.

The letters cover the years between 1931 and 1966. The list of correspondents is immaterial. She wrote pretty much the same letter to each, and to all. The self-absorption is monumental: she speaks of nothing but herself. There is neither real exchange in these letters, nor a sense of any of the people to whom she is writing. Yet the writing is neither selfish, mean-spirited, nor boring. Not a bit of it. The mixture of intelligence, humor, and good nature in these pages is a key to the helplessness of her own self-regard.

She could manage nothing, and she married men who could manage nothing. From earliest youth she had been a trembling, febrile, hapless creature, drunk a good deal of the time, and now she was condemned by a passivity as stubborn as low-grade fever to years of genteel English poverty. She wanders endlessly from one set of rooms to another (in the city, the country, the suburbs) with one helpless husband after another (two of them went to jail for fraud and embezzlement). A pilgrim making an unholy progress, she sighs only for an hour of warmth and peace in which to write, an hour she is never to be permitted. And always there is the cold, the rain, the isolation: "I felt I couldn't take another winter here—the damp cold and loneliness get me down too much. Then I slipped and hurt my arm. Please wish me luck." "I assure you that being down with flu in a cold flat and no telephone just at this moment is *exactly* me. It would happen just that way and no other. . . . Cold shrivels me up and I become incapable of all but shivers and shakes." "My dear—this vast, grim, unheated kitchen, walls steaming with damp, is worth a day in Purgatory, to saw nowt of everything else. . . . The really important difficulty is the place, room, cave, cabin to write in. Our flatlet [has] no vestige of space outside or in and not much privacy. The walls are so thin. It faces a row of low-ceilinged houses like rabbit hutches. One feels so shut in." "Bude is a horribly cold, bleak place and it has rained and hailed all this so called summer. There are no trees. The wind comes straight across the Atlantic at ninety miles an hour, blows off a few roofs along the way then hits you in the chest. . . . I got a bad cold, then my back and legs began to hurt. Then I collapsed. I got all right but so tired—I only wished to sleep and sleep."

This goes on without abatement, year after year, in letter after letter. She apologizes abjectly for complaining, but on she goes. Yet her ability to seduce anew never deserts her. In the middle of an endless whining letter about the cold, the rain, the flu, the floods, there is suddenly a passage like this (written when she was seventy to her estranged daughter): "My dream is to finish my book, get a face lift and a bright red wig. Also a lovely fur coat. Underneath I will wear a purple dress and ropes of pearls. Or what do you say to rags? Then, in all my glory, I will come and see you taking a large suite in a posh hotel. You can tell everyone I'm an eccentric acquaintance. . . . All will be well. *Never fear.*"

She was as tough and honest about writing as she was weak and nerveless about living. She might not have been able to do it—it took her twenty years to complete *Wide Sargasso Sea*—but she never lost sight of what *it* was.

In 1946, trying to sell a book of stories she has no faith in, she writes:

> About my book—the trouble is—it is not good. . . . I tried too hard . . . and was so afraid of offending that I wrote and rewrote the life out of the things. It's all right of course—if anyone believed the truth, that the novel I have half finished [an early version of *Wide Sargasso Sea*] is a very different matter, they'd publish the Sound of the River to give me a helping hand. Sad to say the facts are otherwise. No one does believe in me. . . . And after all when it comes to Facing Facts, I have worked hard for a long time and it's been no good at all—None.

In 1958:

I know very well that I have not all that time—not much perhaps and I know about being forgotten. That must not matter at all. If it [*Sargasso Sea*] is done as truthfully as I can—Only that must matter.

In 1959:

About my book. It is done in the way that patchwork would be done if you had all the colors and all the pieces cut but not yet arranged to make a quilt. No—it is not that I can't bear to let it go—tho' one often feels like that. . . . But I do hesitate about *how* to do it. It must be just right or it will be no good.

She promised her editors the manuscript of *Sargasso Sea* every six months for ten years, and her guilt drove her to write full letters to them, describing the problems she faced in structuring the book. These letters are comprehensive and masterly, the pen held by one whose working authority is not in question.

She adored the idea of writing—"I don't believe in the individual Writer so much as in Writing," she said in 1953, and then later: "All of writing is a huge lake. There are great rivers that feed the lake, like Tolstoy and Dostoevsky. And there are trickles, like Jean Rhys. All that matters is feeding the lake"—and she never complained about the difficulties of a writer's life. The most she

said was, "Max [her husband] thinks that without money and security nothing can be done. *I do not agree at all!* I know otherwise. All the same the time does come when a *little* money a *little*
security a *modicum* of praise does help."

So: on the one hand a neurotic woman driven to alcoholic
withdrawal, on the other a priestess at the shrine of Art. Between
them stands a talented, hardworking writer struggling to make a
book in the shape of her experience.

She had known from the time she was young that men and
women, especially men, fear their own sensuality, that this fear
cuts deep, slicing through intelligence and ordinary decency. If
you were passionate, and you aroused passion in a man, he hated
you—hated and punished and abandoned you She remained
vulnerable to this insight all her life, felt herself a sexual innocent repeatedly crushed by the Ford Madox Fords of life and the
Mr. Mackenzies of her fiction: men of power who were aroused
by her and then turned on her, reviled and humiliated her, left
her "all smashed up."

Clearly, Rhys had a vested interest in her inability to absorb
what one of her editors called "humdrum betrayal." This interest
both retarded and enriched her life, kept her an incapacitated
rag doll but also heightened her sensibility, made her obsessive
over something true that she intuited. Year after year, in book after book, she focused on getting it down right.

The early novels are problematic, interesting and strong but also unattractive and oddly old-fashioned. In these books a single note is struck: a woman in a black velvet dress lies on a narrow bed in a half-darkened room in a pension in a foreign city. When she goes out it is raining. There is nowhere to go and no one to see. She walks the streets in the rain. On her return she stops to pick up a cheap bottle of wine and a man to pay for the wine. She takes them both upstairs. Next morning she is hungover and betrayed.

Into this situation Rhys poured her extraordinary gift for language and form, making of sexual abandonment a parable of modern life. Urban and alienated, her protagonist drinks to kill the pain and sleeps around in the vain hope that the next man will end the isolation. But the situation does not wear well. It feels dated and neurasthenic. The books seem posed, made artificially mysterious by a kind of half knowledge that takes refuge in mythmaking.

In *Wide Sargasso Sea* Antoinette Mason, the Creole heiress who will eventually become the madwoman in Jane Eyre's attic, sleeps with Edward Rochester, the Victoran hidden from himself. Her passion makes come alive in him an answering passion that shocks and frightens him. Repelled by himself, he withdraws from her. His antagonism drives her mad. He takes her to England and locks her in the attic. She escapes and sets fire to the house.

Into *this* situation Rhys poured not only her gift for language and form, but a sense of truth that had come to startling, even unexpected fruition. *Sargasso Sea* is brilliant and redemptive, a novel that rises far above itself, transformed by full awareness. Out of a lifelong preoccupation with what passes between women and men there suddenly emerged a rich interiority: that powerful, trancelike imagining of a "Jamaica" where the bloom of knowledge is radiant malice, where ignorance gives way to a terrible cunning, and people cripple and destroy because they fear themselves. Here, in this novel, Rhys makes of sex-and-respectability the great metaphor she had always known it to be.

In the long letters to her editors one can see it coming. One feels the intimate relation between this writer and this material, how profoundly she draws on original experience, how symbolic of that experience is the split in her between the West Indies of her birth and the England of her maturity. Rhys's lifelong effort to bring the "material" under control begins to seem allegorical.

⌇

There is a tradition in Britain of "unstable" literary women that includes Antonia White, Anna Kavan, Jean Rhys, and Virginia Woolf, each of whom seems to have been permanently stunned by the underlying brutishness of relations between women and men, and each of whom wrote a remarkably interior prose. All were talented, one had genius. All knew that writing demands of the writer that distance be gained on one's inner brooding, and structure imposed. Their various responses to this necessity constitutes a primer on drive and self-discipline. Anna Kavan never rose above obsession and Virginia Woolf never began at less than transcendence. Between them stands Jean Rhys, who worked hard to leave obsession behind, to disentangle and pull from herself the long line of slowly clarifying thought that justifies a writer's life. Her letters do not explain the effort but they register it admirably, in all its exhaustion and all its nobility.

Ruthless Intimacies

I T W A S T H E T O N E of *Sons and Lovers,* not the subject matter, that came as a shock when the novel was published in 1913.
The directness of the writing established the erotic hold that the
mother and the son had on each other. To see it laid down on the
page was amazing. But ten minutes after the book had been published, everyone who could read said, "Of course. How could it
be otherwise?" Two things had happened at once: a writer able
to speak had appeared in a world ready to hear and, as timing is
all, that which had been felt was now understood.

From Oedipus to Freud, our idea of the struggle to be in the
world has taken its character from the conflict between fathers
and sons, a history of violence and urgency that for centuries has
stirred the imaginative act of self description. However fraught
the conflict, essentially it is without ambiguity. The father, compelled as he is to subdue the son, would despise him if he stayed.

The son, anguished as he is over fighting the father, remains undivided in his need to go. He wants the world, and if he must tear flesh and maim spirit to get it, so be it. Life is born out of force and denial at the hands of one's intimates. This is knowledge to be taken in manfully. In fact, the taking in of this knowledge is precisely what has always been called manful.

Henry James—through the women he created—was the first modern writer to explain that in the matter of the world, we are divided against ourselves, at once both attracted and repelled. We advance on the world, we shrink from the world; we desire the world, we fear the world. It is a love affair compromised by the sick excitement of mixed feelings.

D. H. Lawrence could taste the dividedness in his mouth. He knew the obsessiveness between himself and his mother was laced through with fear and desire on a large scale. It was she who provoked his longing, made his spirit bleed, roused him to energy and anxiety. He could see that it was *this* relationship, not the one with the father, that was the crucial one in the matter of the world and the divided self. Still, Lawrence was a man and *Sons and Lovers* a coming-of-age novel. It was a given that enraged, depressed, unwilling as the protagonist might be, he would nonetheless be propelled *out*. True, the mother must die before the son is free to go, but at no point in the novel is there any real possibility that the son will take rooms with the widowed mother and settle down to an unlived life.

In this century our understanding, both of the struggle and of the conflict, has taken a quantum leap. Another view of the matter has been clarifying itself over the past sixty years, one that has warranted a shift in interest from fathers and sons to mothers and daughters. The necessity, it now seems, is not so much to kill our fathers as it is to separate from our mothers, and it is the daughters who must do the separating. This view includes but subsumes the testimony of mothers and sons, and restores us to fruitful ambiguity. It's the ambiguity that belongs to the women—and it, too, has a fictional history as well as an actual one. Nowhere in literature is there a female equivalent of the protagonist locked in successful struggle, either with the father or the mother, for the sake of the world. But a remarkable number of novels exist that detail an unsuccessful struggle, and these are richly informing.

In 1924 a novel was published in England that bore a striking resemblance to *Sons and Lovers*, one large difference being that its major characters were all women and its resolution far different. It was called *The Unlit Lamp* and was written by Radclyffe Hall, later (and better) known as the author of the scandalous *Well of Loneliness*. *The Unlit Lamp* tells the story of Joan Ogden, an intelligent girl growing up in a shabby-genteel household in a coastal town called Seabourne at the turn of the century. Mr. Ogden is a failure and Mrs. Ogden is a snob. Mr. Ogden rules the house in red-faced Victorian bluster and Mrs. Ogden retreats into permanent ill health. Her only pleasure is her daughter Joan whose sympathetic understanding becomes her comfort and then her necessity. The daughter's love is a swamp of romantic pity. The mother sinks shamelessly into the girl's attachment and, in the great tradition of ordinary family life, these two become hideously addicted to one another.

Enter Elizabeth Rodney: twenty-six years old, sister to a forty-five-year-old Seabourne bachelor. Elizabeth has gone to Cambridge but now, educated as she is, what is there for her to do, alone in the world, in England in 1895? She can either teach in a boarding school or become a governess or a paid companion. Of course, she *could* go up to London and take her chances; other "new women" are doing it, but. . . . She drifts back to her brother's house and is engaged by Mrs. Ogden to teach the fourteen-year-old Joan and her younger sister.

Joan Ogden is exceptional in Seabourne. Her mind is vigorous, straightforward, brave; her spirit longs for emotional adventure; her body is on the verge of deep feeling. She crops her hair, wears tailored clothes, takes long open strides. Elizabeth sees in Joan the promise that marked her own early life. She also sees Mrs. Ogden's indifference to Joan's gifts. All the mother wants is assurance that the girl's allegiance will never shift from love of her to love of her own independence. Elizabeth determines to save the girl from the mother. The subject of the novel is the split within Joan herself, embodied by the claims laid equally on her by Elizabeth and Mary Ogden (Elizabeth: "Come live with me in London. You'll go to Cambridge, become a doctor, become anything you want. If you don't get away from here you'll not have a life." Mary: "Don't leave me, darling. You're all I have in the world. Without you I'll die.").

In the end Joan does not leave her mother. Everyone else gets away from Seabourne — her sister, her friends, Elizabeth — but not she. Her feeling for her mother drags her down, makes her vulnerable to guilt and pity, shrivels her nerve. "I can't do it," she begs Elizabeth. But Elizabeth turns on her heel: for the failure of courage there is no sympathy, only consequence.

The achievement of *The Unlit Lamp* is its psychological acumen: the plausibility of mood shift, the shrewdness of pacing. What the reader tastes in her mouth here, with Joan Ogden, is the way it feels when you *can't* make it, when you don't enter the world.

As in *Sons and Lovers*, the attachment between the mother and the child is openly erotic. Joan's overwrought brooding, Mary's loverlike appeals, the endless preoccupaion of each with the other's response to any given moment or circumstance — this is romantic fixation conveyed in a language startling for its unmediated directness. One reads in astonishment what these two say to one another, do to one another, and all the while one is murmuring, "Of course. How could it be otherwise?" The writer knows what really goes on between a mother and a daughter when the daughter wants to live not the given life but a free life. For that the mother must fight the daughter, and the daughter must fight her own fearful self. They're on the ropes, these

two, locked together in pain and rage. This is a matter of intimacy, not love. Such intimacy is ruthless. Ruthless intimacy is
erotic.

⁓

From the beginning of the century there have been novels dominated by female characters who do not act, but who reveal strong
knowledge of the struggle to leave home. In these novels
mother-daughter relations are hard, not sentimental. Among
the most impressive is May Sinclair's *Mary Olivier*, published in
1919, six years after *Sons and Lovers* and five before *The Unlit
Lamp*. Sinclair, then a writer of twenty years' standing, was an
Edwardian who converted to modernism. Touched by Freud
and the imagists, she was stirred to write a remarkable autobio-
graphical novel. Ostensibly about Victorian family life, it was in
fact about her inability to leave her mother.

The period is 1896 to 1910, the place the English countryside,
the characters Mamma, Papa, three sons, and a daughter. The
daughter is intelligent and talented: she plays the piano brilliantly, reads her brothers' schoolbooks in secret, teaches herself
Greek. The mother likes the daughter only when she is a tiny
child, and acts like a girl; when she begins to exhibit an independent mind, the mother mocks her. The girl never recovers from
the mother's scorn. She becomes fixated on its alleviation. Very
nearly, the girl realizes her mother's love is the go-ahead signal
she requires to enter the world; that is, to occupy "the enormous,

perfect crystal" of her own thinking mind. Very nearly, the mother realizes that to withhold her love is to bind the girl to her forever. In the end, the men all disappear—the father dies of alcoholism, the sons go off to Canada and India, lovers are sent away—and the two women are left alone, facing each other in a silent house on a provincial street at the turn of the century. Only death will terminate this unholy devotion.

Again, the tone is everything. The tone, and the girl's understanding from earliest adolescence of her attachment to her mother. At fourteen, losing her own faith, Mary watches Mrs. Olivier on her knees, singing hymns:

> She could see the stiff, slender muscles in her mother's neck. The weak, plaintive voice tore at her heart. Its thin, sweet notes unnerved her. . . . She could feel already the chill of an intolerable separation. She could give up Jesus, the lover of her soul, but she could not give up her mother. She couldn't live separated from the weak, plaintive voice that tore at her. She couldn't do it.

At sixteen, Mary sits down at the piano to play Chopin:

> She exulted in her power over the Polonaise. Nothing could touch you, nothing could hurt you while you played. If only you could go on playing forever. . . . Her mother came in from the garden. "Mary," she said, "if you will play, you must play gently." "But Mamma—I can't. It goes like that." "Then

don't play it. You can be heard all over the village." "Bother the village. I don't care if I'm heard all over everywhere!" She went on playing. But it was no use. She struck a wrong note. Her hands trembled and lost their grip. They stiffened, dropped from the keys. She sat and stared idiotically at the white page, at the black bars swaying. She had forgotten how to play Chopin.

A few years later on the night before her father's funeral, Mary lies down beside her mother to hold her in her arms: "How small she was. You could feel her little shoulder blades, weak and fine under your fingers, like a child's. You could break them. To be happy with her either you or she had to be broken. To be helpless and little like a child."

The beloved son returns from India and Mary tells him, "Ever since I began to grow up I felt there was something about Mamma that would kill me if I let it. I've had to fight for every single thing I've ever wanted." The brother, puzzled, looks at her. "Fight little Mamma?" he asks. "No. Myself," she replies. "The bit of me that claws on to her and can't get away."

At the very last, too late for either of them, the frail mother clutches at the forty-year-old virgin daughter and confides: "I was jealous of you, Mary. And I was afraid for my life you'd find it out." The exhausted daughter nods and remains silent. She long ago understood it all.

In 1927, when Virginia Woolf wrote *To the Lighthouse*, she provided the story with a more sophisticated psychology. Describing an intellectual Victorian family at the seashore, Woolf told a modernist tale of the extension and withdrawal of human sympathies. The novel was read primarily as an account of male will and female accommodation—Mr. and Mrs. Ramsay became emblematic of the arrangement behind a successful marriage—but the interesting relationship in the book is the one between Lily Briscoe and Mrs. Ramsay. Theirs is a dreamlike inversion of the angry passions that dominate *The Unlit Lamp* and *Mary Olivier*. *To the Lighthouse* raises with less heat and rather more light the question that animates those earlier novels—whether to be in the world or to become one's mother; supply sympathy to men or be odd, lonely, unmarried: an artist.

Lily Briscoe—painter, spinster, friend of the family—is a surrogate daughter, Mrs. Ramsay an idealization of the woman's life against which Lily pits her own. Woolf's refusal to make Lily an actual daughter has its own poignant consequence, but it provides the distance necessary to penetrate the matter more deeply.

Lily stands on the lawn, looking at a flower against the wall of the house:

> The jacmanna was bright violet; the wall staring white. Then beneath the color there was the shape. She could see it all so clearly, so commandingly, when she looked: it was when she took her brush in hand that the whole thing changed. It was in that moment's flight between the picture and her canvas

that the demons set on her who often brought her to the verge of tears and made this passage from conception to work as dreadful as any down a dark passage for a child. . . . And it was then too, as she began to paint, that there forced themselves upon her other things, her own inadequacy, her insignificance, keeping house for her father off the Brompton road, and had much ado to control her impulse to fling herself (thank Heaven she had always resisted so far) at Mrs. Ramsay's knee and say to her—but what could one say to her? "I'm in love with you?"

Mrs. Ramsay, for her part, frets in the privacy of her rare solitary moments:

It was odd; and she believed it to be true; that with all his gloom and desperation [Mr. Ramsay] was happier, more hopeful on the whole, than she was. . . . He had always his work to fall back on. Not that she herself was "pessimistic" as he accused her of being. Only she thought life. . . . Life, she thought—but she did not finish her thought. She took a look at life, for she had a clear sense of it there, something real, something private, which she shared neither with her children nor with her husband. A sort of transaction went on between them, in which she was on one side, and life was on another, and she was always trying to get the better of it, as it was of her; and sometimes they parleyed (when she sat alone); there were, she remembered, great reconciliation scenes; but for the most part, oddly enough, she must admit that she felt this thing that she called life terrible, hostile, and quick to pounce on you if you gave it a chance.

These passages are part of a silent exchange between Lily and Mrs. Ramsay that dominates the book. Lily has her work, but she trembles before the reality her own powers bestow on her and wants to fall back into the Mrs. Ramsay inside herself. Mrs. Ramsay, at the adored center of the family, has the safety of her position as wife and mother, but she is depressed, angry, an abstraction to herself. Each needs the other to complete the dynamic that runs like a current beneath the surface of the prose. The question being asked is, Where is the world? Without or within? And the characters who become the question are Lily and Mrs. Ramsay. *To the Lighthouse* persuades us that no man (except, perhaps, one in a James novel) could embody the metaphor behind the question as well as these anxious, intelligent women. Now, sixty years later, an interested reader is tempted to add that maybe only a mother and a daughter will do.

Ten years ago Edna O'Brien published a short story called "A Rose in the Heart of New York," one of many centered on country women in Ireland, lost in their brutish marriages, living out their years in gloomy village houses. "A Rose" is more of a meditation than a story. A woman gives birth to a baby girl in a farmhouse outside of the village. The father drinks and is violent. The mother and the child cling together. The girl grows up, goes to school, gets married, gets divorced, goes to England. Back in

Ireland, the parents endure. Within herself, the girl, now a grown woman, turns away from her mother. Feeling guilty, she tries to compensate by taking the mother to a seaside hotel, where they quarrel, and part in anger. Before they can reconcile the mother dies. None of this is dramatized. The subject of the piece—the feeling between the mother and the daughter—is to be found in the writing, not in the narrative. Language becomes the thing itself—language, and a startling sexuality. "A Rose in the Heart of New York" is more erotically disturbing than any of O'Brien's love-affair-with-a-married-man stories. Certainly, it is more primitive.

The mother sobs as she is giving birth, "gripping the coverlet and remembering that between those selfsame, much-patched sheets, she had been prized apart, again and again, with not a word to her, not a little endearment, only rammed through and told to open up." The child born in violation is idolized; she returns the feeling. The mother and the child absorb each other's necessity:

> They were together, always together.... Her mother's knuckles were her knuckles, her mother's veins were her veins, her mother's lap was a second heaven, her mother's forehead a copybook onto which she traced A B C D, her mother's body was a recess that she would wander inside forever and ever, a sepulcher growing deeper and deeper [They] slept side by side, entwined like twigs of trees or the end of the sugar tongs.... The girl had no friends, she didn't need any. Her cup was full. Her mother was the cup, the

cupboard, the sideboard with all the things in it, the bog with the wishing well in it, the sea with the oysters and the corpses in it, her mother a gigantic sponge, a habitation in which she longed to sink and disappear forever and ever. Yet she was afraid to sink, caught in that hideous trap between fear of sinking and fear of swimming.

Suddenly, the girl grows up and seems not to think of her mother for years at a time. Then her marriage ends, and she leaves Ireland to make a new life.

She was staggered by the assaults of memory—a bowl with her mother's menstrual cloth soaking in it and her sacrilegious idea that if lit it could resemble the heart of Christ. . . . The mother had a splinter under her nail and the girl felt her own nail being lifted up, felt hurt to the quick, or felt her mother's sputum, could taste it like a dish. She was possessed by these thoughts in the library where she worked day in and day out. . . . They were more than thoughts, they were the presence of this woman whom she resolved to kill. Yes, she would have to kill. . . . She thought of choking or drowning. . . . She saw herself holding big suffocating pillows or a bolster, in the secrecy of the room where it had all begun. Her mother turned into bursting red pipes, into brown dishcloths, into swamps of black-brown blooded water. Her mother turned into a streetwalker and paraded. Her mother was taking down her knickers in public, squatting to do awful things, her mother was drifting down a well in a big bucket, crying for help, but no help was forthcoming.

Later, at the hotel, "the mother said there was no such thing as love between the sexes and that it was all bull. She reaffirmed that there was only one kind of love and that was a mother's love for her child. There passed between them such a moment, not a moment of sweetness, not a moment of reaffirmation, but a moment dense with hate—one hating and the other receiving it like rays."

The shock, inevitably, in all these writings comes from the open declaration of murderous feeling. We accept rage and ruthlessness as a matter of course in erotic attachment, but here we are being made to see that *all* intimacies are ruthless—and all eroticized. When the intimacy is with a parent—especially with a parent of the same sex—the passionate element remains, as it must, disguised, but the astonishing anger and depression it generates is surely the measure of fearful and subterranean feeling. How could it be otherwise? This is the intimacy that will bind us all our lives, holding us forever to the task implicit in all love relations: how to connect yet not merge, how to respond yet not be absorbed, how to detach but not withdraw.

Sons and Lovers was written out of insight possessed in the nerve endings. Lawrence knew as much as any man in his historical moment could know, and he took us further than we had been before. After him the world grew larger.

Today the most ignorant among us knows that murder will not accomplish separation. You can't kill your mother because there is no mother to kill. It's the mother within who's doing all the damage. That's a piece of shared wisdom that the culture knows down to its fingertips. Some woman who writes is about to take *our* wisdom further than it's been, and when she does, the world will seem bigger yet.

Willa Cather

WILLA CATHER once observed that in all families the

struggle to have anything of one's own, to be one's self at all, creates a strain that keeps everybody almost at the breaking point. . . . Even in harmonious families there is this double life: the group life, which is the one we can observe . . . and, underneath, another—secret and passionate and intense— which is the real life that stamps the faces and gives character to the voices of our friends. Always in his mind each member [of the family] is escaping, running away, trying to break the net which circumstances and his own affections have woven about him. . . . One realizes that human relationships are the tragic necessity of human life: every ego is half the time greedily seeking them, and half the time pulling away from them.

Years later, Katherine Anne Porter wrote of these words:

This is masterly and water-clear and autobiography enough for me: my mind goes with tenderness to the big lonely slow-moving girl who happened to be an artist coming back from reading Latin and Greek with an old storekeeper [in the town], helping with the housework, then sitting by the fireplace to talk down an assertive brood of brothers and sisters, practicing her art on them, refusing to be lost among them — the longest-winged one who would fly free at last.

She was born in 1873 in Virginia, into a family of highly literate country people (both grandmothers knew Latin and Greek), people who took as their birthright the idea that it was civilized to be educated and have a sense of culture; and that to be civilized was the highest good. When she was nine years old, the family moved to Red Cloud, Nebraska. The father proved a disastrous farmer. After a year on the open plain, the family took a house in town. Mr. Cather became an insurance agent. The children grew up healthy, loving, competitive. Everyone knew Willa's intelligence was remarkable, and when the time came, she was sent to the state university at Lincoln. In Lincoln she distinguished herself as a brilliant eccentric. She was a large girl, ungainly and overdirect; a passionate reader and talker with unreliable social skills, often blurting out some indiscreet bit of scorn. One other thing about her made people apprehensive. She seemed to develop huge crushes on women — classmates, acquaintances, faculty wives — that were intense and long-lasting. The object of her necessity would inevitably demur, and Willa would become aggressively unhappy. People grew alarmed. Then turned cold and distant.

By the time she graduated, she knew she could write. Music and theater had always meant a great deal to her, and she was thrilled to be taken on by the Lincoln newspaper as a reviewer. She did wonderfully well, so well that in a year or two a job offer came from a Pittsburgh magazine, and off she went. There was never a thought of her going home to Red Cloud. Everyone knew she'd gone out into the world the minute she left for school, and now there was nothing for it but to go further into the world. From Lincoln to Pittsburgh to New York. The bigger the city, the more she loved it. An urban natural: with each leap in population she experienced a leap in heart.

In Pittsburgh she became a professional journalist, and there, too, she met Isabelle McClung: daughter of a judge, rich, beautiful, cultivated. Willa fell in love instantly and irrevocably. Isabelle returned affection, not passion. But each became and remained for the other an incarnation of perfect communion. The connection lasted forty years. It is possible but not very likely, I think, that they slept together.

In 1903 Cather met Sam McClure, editor of *McClure's Magazine*, and a book publisher as well. McClure urged her to send him her stories. She did, and he summoned her to New York, begged her to work for him, told her he would publish anything she wrote. He was as good as his word. She came to New York, and in 1905 he brought out her first collection of stories, *The Troll*

Garden. But the book went unnoticed, and the silence so frightened her that she settled down to editing.

Under McClure, Cather became a skilled editor and magazine writer, but she quickly came to see what working at the magazine was doing to her. As James Woodress, one of Cather's biographers, writes, "The reading of so many poorly written manuscripts had a deadening effect [on her]. She knew that some people could do it, but it [had come to give] her a kind of dread of everything made out of words. She felt diluted and weakened by it all the time as though she were in a tepid bath and could no longer stand heat or cold." Yet, she could not bring herself to leave. At the age of thirty-five she felt frightened of writing: "a newborn baby every time, always naked and shivering and without any bones."

But against the fear and the anxiety, the drive was gathering. Slowly, there accumulated in her the compulsion to write out of the experience of her inner life. To discover for herself what it was she knew about human beings, really knew, and to spend her life exploring that territory. What would her true subject be? What would make the words come alive under her pen? What did she know on the surface of things, and what did she know down to the bone? To think about what she felt: that would be her life's work.

In 1912 she left McClure's for good (she had tried a number of times before but could not manage it), settled into an apartment on Bank Street with her friend Edith Lewis (a copyeditor at the magazine), and began to live the remarkably quiet life that produced an unbroken flow of novels, stories, and essays over the next thirty years. Greenwich Village in the twenties and thirties was exploding with Freud, Marx, and Emma Goldman, but for Cather it was all happening at a great distance. In the country of her life these were border disturbances. By 1918 she had written *O Pioneers!*, *The Song of the Lark*, and *My Ántonia*. From the beginning, her books brought recognition and money. She spent the winter in New York, the summer in Nebraska and New Mexico. In the fall or spring she often went to New Hampshire. A number of times she traveled to Europe. Music remained a passion, and many of her friends were musical. She grew handsome as she grew older but, essentially, remained the large smiling plain-faced woman she had always been, wearing schoolgirl middy blouses into her fifties, unfashionable and immature until it was safe, in her famous sixties, to put on the beautiful silk dresses she *did* know how to wear.

Much has been made of the fact that she lived forty years with Edith Lewis, but if ever there was a Boston marriage this surely was it. Lewis was her friend, companion, and secretary; there is little reason to believe they were lovers, and much to conclude they were not. To begin with, Cather loved Isabelle McClung with a romantic yearning she expressed until her death (even though Isabelle had married in 1916). Then there are the letters between her and Lewis: all business, not a shred of erotic intimacy to be found in them. Finally, there is the work itself, stripped as it is of all grown-up desire. Of what actually happens between people who have experienced passion, there is not a word in Cather to indicate she had ever had sexual relations.

She loved women. There is no question of that. But to do it? Take off her clothes and lie down with them? Become a lesbian? That, I think, she could not do, and did not do. I can imagine her imagining open-faced Nebraska shrinking from her were she to become openly homosexual, and she shrank from that rejection. Easier, by far, to remain celibate. Celibate and civilized.

This was her vital piece of arrest, her significant damage. Because she was an artist, disability powered imaginative insight. It made her see the thing she might not otherwise have seen, and it made her love what no other woman writer in America had loved half so well. She didn't hate sex, she was just afraid of it. Sensuality remained alive in her, and she stayed responsive to its demands. She didn't close down and she didn't freeze up; she sublimated. In her books she makes love to life through her descriptions of the American land, and through the adolescent adoration that she allows boy narrators to lavish on some of her most suggestive characters (Ántonia, for one; Marian Forrester, the Lost Lady, for another). That's why Cather has always seemed such an innocent—because Nebraska and New Mexico got the sex, as well as the boys who pine and yearn but can never act. So we all read *Death Comes for the Archbishop* or *My Ántonia* in high school and found ourselves immensely stirred without knowing why.

Death Comes for the Archbishop tells the story of the French missionary priest who brought Catholicism to New Mexico, and *My Ántonia* that of immigrant settlers on the Nebraska plain, but each novel is dominated by the strength and beauty of the land. The power of Cather's descriptions — they are not of nature as such — lies in the feeling for the land as it enters into her characters, and that feeling is sexual. One is stirred in the groin as well as the heart reading Willa Cather on the American Southwest.

⁊

But what of the thing she saw that she would not otherwise have seen? Because she could not have a sexual life, she understood that to be oneself was not a given. All around and everywhere, in the quietest of lives, the narrowest of circumstances, she saw that people struggled to be themselves. In the most harmonious of families, as she put it, an oppression of spirit seemed to overtake people, and she knew that it was because they were feeling stifled. In many marriages, she observed, especially those that had been great love matches to begin with, one sometimes saw a shocking rage beneath the polite surface, and she knew it was because one or both were now feeling dead within themselves. She saw that in remote and provincial places, among ignorant, small-minded people, there were always men and women who suffered visibly. In all human beings, there is what she called an essential spirit, an expressive, inviolable self. She knew it was the task of every life to fashion an existence that would feed the expressive self.

This was the thing she saw that she might otherwise not have seen. It became her subject, her metaphor, her lifelong preoccupation. For thirty years she wrote stories and novels in which human beings struggle with the question of how to be themselves. If her characters struggle successfully, somehow or other they come to glory. If not, if the inviolable self is denied or ignored, abused or pushed out of shape, the character comes to grief. Because Cather lived without knowledge of sexual love, in her plots she often made marriage the easy enemy of the beleaguered self. But in her prose — in its rich, clear depth and its remarkable capaciousness — she knows better. She knows this struggle has to do with the deepest of fears; that to be oneself is a lonely and a fearful thing and, in the end, we each manufacture, or refuse to manufacture, the courage necessary for the task at hand.

The Song of the Lark, published in 1915, was her manifesto. In this novel she stakes out the territory for the first time — and loads the issue shamelessly. The story is a great romance. Thea Kronborg, the musically gifted daughter of Swedish immigrants, grows up in Moonstone, Colorado, in the 1880s. The doctor in the town, an intelligent, unhappy man recognizes the sensitivity of the child and becomes her friend and mentor. In time he helps her leave Moonstone for Chicago, where she will study with a pianist of reputation. In Chicago Thea endures poverty, loneliness, and terrible uncertainty, but the will that drives her is overpowering. The piano teacher makes the crucial discovery: it's her voice that's the real talent, not her piano playing. He shows her the way forward. A wealthy musical dilettante falls in love with her; he also helps her to see herself more truly. Exhausted and confused, Thea makes a trip to the Southwest, where, in the great canyons of the American earth, she undergoes a mystical experience and knows what she must do. She returns to Chicago, wires the doctor for money, goes to Germany to study singing, and, by the end of the book, she has become a rising prima donna in the New York opera: intent and narrowed down, staring into the glory-filled, demanding years ahead of her. She is, of course, alone.

The first time the piano teacher hears Thea sing, he's astonished. Her voice is "like a wild bird that had flown into his studio. . . . No one knew that it had come, or even that it existed; least of all the strange crude girl in whose throat it beat its passionate wings." Later, he muses, "under her crudeness and brusque hardness, he felt there was a nature quite different, of which he never got so much as a hint except when she was at the piano, or when she sang. It was toward this hidden creature that he was trying, for his own pleasure, to find his way. . . . she stirred him more than anything she did could adequately explain." Then, when he tries to make Thea understand that she must sing, he says to her:

> My girl, you are very talented. You could be a pianist, a good one. . . . You are not by nature, I think, a pianist. You would

never find yourself. In the effort to do so, I'm afraid your playing would become warped, eccentric. . . . I believe that the
strongest need of your nature is to find yourself, to emerge as
yourself. Until I heard you sing, I wondered how you were to
do this, but it has grown clearer to me every day. . . . You have
brains enough and talent enough. But to do what you will
want to do, it takes more than these—it takes vocation. Now,
I think you have vocation. But for the voice, not for the
piano.

Still later, Fred Ottenburg, the rich man who loves her but,
like all the men in this book, wants Thea to have her life, says
to her,

Don't you know most of the people in the world are not indi-
viduals at all? . . . A lot of girls go to boarding-school together,
come out the same season, dance at the same parties, are
married off in groups, have their babies at about the same
time, send their children to school together, and so the human crop renews itself. Such women know as much about
the reality of the forms they go through as they know about
the wars they learned the dates of. They get their most personal experiences out of novels and plays. . . . You are not
that sort of person. . . . You will always break through into
the realities.

It is from passages like these—vivid, sustained, dominating—
that *The Song of the Lark* draws its power. Cather makes a great

romance of the loneliness of the artist's vocation, into which she pours her own defiant necessity, but that is not her subject at all. Her subject is the conviction that in pursuit of the deepest self there is glory, and in the absence of that pursuit there is emptiness.

Willa Cather left twelve novels, four collections of stories, two volumes of nonfiction, and two volumes of poetry. It seems to me there are traces of this preoccupation throughout, but the novels in which it collects with sufficient skill and force of concentration to produce remarkable work are *The Professor's House*, *My Mortal Enemy*, and *Lucy Gayheart*, the first two written in the mid-twenties, the third in the mid-thirties.

My Mortal Enemy, a novella famous for its startling economy, is a swift, deep thrust into the flesh of an unhappy marriage. It tells the story of a beautiful girl of temperament and intelligence who is disinherited when she marries—against her rich uncle's wishes—the man with whom she is infatuated. Love proves shallow, marriage long-lasting, and Myra Henshawe's life a disaster. When she is dying in circumstances of horrifying shabbiness, her helpless husband begs her to believe he will rescue her yet. She smoothes his hair and says, "No, my poor Oswald, you'll never stagger far under the bulk of me. . . . It's been the ruin of us both. We've destroyed each other. I should have stayed with my uncle. It was money I needed. We've thrown our lives away. . . . We were never really happy. I am a greedy, selfish, worldly woman; I wanted success and a place in the world. Now

I'm old and ill and a fright, but among my own kind I'd still have my circle." Close to the end, nearly unconscious and muttering to herself, she cries out: "I could bear to suffer. . . . So many have suffered. But why must it be like this? . . . Why must I die like this, alone with my mortal enemy?"

Myra's mortal enemy is not the marriage but her own lost self. In her element Myra Henshawe is a marvelous creature; out of it she's frightening—she *is* all the nasty things she says she is. The novel does not judge Myra; it only takes an unsentimental view of what happens when a marriage made in ignorance distorts someone of strong character. It's the question of not knowing oneself that interests Cather.

Lucy Gayheart is Thea Kronborg with less talent and no drive at all. She falters quickly out in the world, and just as quickly dies of her own cowardice. The loveliest and most promising girl in her small midwestern town, Lucy is courted by Harry Gordon, the rich man's son. But Lucy can play the piano, and is determined on a larger life. She goes to Chicago to study, but instead meets and falls in love with Clement Sebastian, a handsome baritone who indulges his own romantic fantasies with her. Sebastian goes to Europe for the summer, promising to return to Lucy in September, but he dies in a boating accident; (anyway, as it turns out, he's married). Lucy falls apart in Chicago and then returns to her hometown, where she is scorned by the man she had earlier scorned. She passes from grief to despair to incapacity, and finally dies by drowning, just as the man through whom she had hoped to live had died.

The pages of this book are drenched with the misery of Lucy's failure of nerve and the penetrating gloom of small-town life to which she is consigned. But Cather's feeling for her story is so fine by now (1935) that it is possible to ignore her melodramatic plot and respond wholly to the intelligence guiding the atmospheric situation.

When Lucy hears Sebastian sing in Chicago, she knows she is listening to the sound of someone who has given himself entirely to his work. She understands in that moment the courage that is required of her, and understands also that she's not up to it. Cather writes,

> Lucy had come home and up the stairs, into this room, tired and frightened with a feeling that some protecting barrier was gone—a window had been broken that let in the cold and darkness of the night.... Some people's lives are affected by what happens to their person and their property; but for others fate is what happens to their feelings and their thoughts—that and nothing more.

In Chicago, waiting for Sebastian to return from Europe, Lucy remembers other summers when she had gone home, and the realization that she is caught begins to quicken in her: there is no going back.

> This summer there would be no slowing down to the village pace. No walking about the town for hours and hours in the moonlight ... everything so still about her, everything so

wide awake within her. . . . She wondered that her heart hadn't burst in those long vacations, when there was no human image she could hold up against the summer night; when she was alone out there, looking up at the moon from the bottom of a well. She loved her own little town, but it was a heart-breaking love, like loving the dead who cannot answer back.

In describing Harry Gordon's pain at the sight of Lucy once more on the streets of the town, a sight he cannot avoid, Cather observes,

In little towns, lives roll along so close to one another; loves and hates beat about, their wings almost touching. On the sidewalks along which everybody comes and goes, you must, if you walk abroad at all, at some time pass within a few inches of the man who cheated and betrayed you, or the woman you desire more than anything else in the world. Her skirt brushes against you. You say good morning, and go on. It is a close shave. Out in the world the escapes are not so narrow.

In the end, the failure to become makes Lucy run out of even the narrowest of escapes.

The Professor's House is Cather's strongest novel. Very little happens; the agent of change is consciousness. The professor becomes slowly aware that, at the age of fifty-two, he is suicidal for the simple reason that the life he has constructed has left him dead at the center. Without feeling in vital places. Unable to obtain nourishment for the mind or spirit. He wants not so much to die as to not go on living.

Godfrey St. Peter is an academic historian who has lived his entire adult life in a small university town on the shores of Lake Michigan. He married early, for love, a woman of beauty and taste, and with her raised two lovely daughters. His career also prospered: he's been rewarded with recognition and money for an eight-volume history he wrote on the early Spanish explorers in the American Southwest.

These books were written in the attic study of an eccentric old house the family occupied throughout the years the girls were growing up. Now the professor's wife has had built, with his prize money, a new house, at some distance from the old one, equipped with all the modern comforts the old one lacked. The professor finds himself uneasy in this house, says he can only work in the old attic study, and insists on retaining the empty house for a year. During this year he gradually comes to realize that his marriage is loveless, that he cannot generate new work, and that his life is now all form and no substance. He resolves never to move into the new house.

Oh, one other complication: Tom Outland. Some years before the time in which the story takes place, Tom Outland—a cowpuncher from New Mexico who studied Latin on his own— had presented himself at the professor's door and announced his desire for a university education. He'd been integrated into the St. Peters' lives almost immediately, and the professor had come to love him. This boy was the student of his dreams, the one with sufficient power of mind and imagination to take in, make use of, the professor's knowledge and wisdom. Tom becomes a scientist, makes a discovery of commercial usefulness, falls in love with the professor's older daughter, makes her his heir, and goes off to fight in the First World War, from which he does not return. The Outland Patent makes the daughter and her subsequent husband rich. The professor is left with a journal in which Tom tells the story of how he and another cowpuncher had made an archeological find in New Mexico, digging out of an unexplored mesa, and uncovering the cliff dwellings of an ancient and superior race of Indians (this tale is based on the discovery of Mesa Verde).

Now, in the summer of crisis, the professor reads the journal again. "Tom Outland's Story" — a novella-length section within *The Professor's House* — is an extraordinary evocation of what the American Southwest meant to Willa Cather. Tom literally *becomes* as he climbs higher into the mesa, deeper into an awed perception of humanity's great effort at civilization. He realizes that now he must make of his own life the effort the Indians made on the mesa, that life is an endless process of making that effort. He has arrived at the meaning of struggle. The professor, reading Tom's journal, sees that he has never had the wisdom of this boy. His own life has been uninformed, without deliberation or real choice. He has never arrived at the point of struggle.

The professor—passive, vain, self-absorbed—is not an appealing character, but Cather enters into his situation. She puts herself inside this man; makes him turn his existence, from incident to incident, over in his mind throughout this crucial year; makes him look at his wife first with contempt (Lillian's "good taste" is iron in his mouth), then with pity (suddenly, he feels her isolation), and finally with indifference; he studies his relationship with each of his daughters, with his old colleague, with his students, with his sons-in-law; he lets himself be flooded by memories of Tom Outland until he understands what Tom has signified for him. The novel is as unintegrated as the professor's life, but the writing is unforgettable: fully mature and unmistakably American.

⌒

When I read Willa Cather I sometimes find myself thinking of two writers who were working at the same time as she, also women for whom the terrors of sexual life were richly suggestive—Jean Rhys and Virginia Woolf—and it's then that I realize how much the tone and perspective Cather brings to her work, the way she frames the problem, the spirit of approach, the underlying mood of expectation mark her as distinctly American.

Imagine: in 1925 Jean Rhys was writing *Quartet*, Virginia Woolf published *Mrs. Dalloway*, and Willa Cather *The Professor's House*. Woolf and Rhys were a pair of Englishwomen much influenced by modernism—one making of sexuality a bleak urban parable, the other moving out of the promise and failure of human sympathy onto a vast field of inner vision. Cather meanwhile, that incomparable daughter of transcendentalism, made a homely contemplation on the necessity of achieving wholeness of being.

In 1925 Woolf and Rhys seemed sophisticated, Cather an American provincial. When Jean Rhys wrote "he left me all smashed up," she meant, "life and history inevitably leave one all smashed up." Cather, on the other hand, wrote as one who saw herself pitted against the elements in a fair fight, and there was no question but that the fight was worthy. Not only worthy, obligatory. At all times one's life is worth having.

In the most unsentimental of Cather's moods there is neither despair nor loss of energy. This seems to me American through and through. Not only American but very much of our moment. The long bitterness of modern alienation feels worked out just now. The greatest of the talents of anomie still holds our attention, but the smaller ones make us restless. Today Jean Rhys seems dated, Virginia Woolf important, and Willa Cather wise.

Hannah Arendt and
Martin Heidegger

WHAT IT COMES DOWN TO is this. If you don't understand your feelings, you're pulled around by them all your life. If you understand but are unable to integrate them, you're destined for years of pain. If you deny and despise their power, you are lost. This is what the great characters in Hardy and Ibsen are about: women and men in the very grip. In Hardy they struggle unsuccessfully, and come to sorrow. In Ibsen they repress and deny, and they are doomed.

The story of Hannah Arendt and Martin Heidegger belongs to the dramatists, not the critics. It is a tale of emotional connection made early, never fully grasped, then buried alive in feeling the protagonists kept hidden from themselves. Such feeling is like a weed pushing up through concrete. When the hurricane is over, and the world is littered with destruction, it is still waving in the wind.

Hannah Arendt became Martin Heidegger's student at the University of Marburg in 1924. She was eighteen years old. He was thirty-five and already famous in university circles. (Three years later, when *Being and Time* was published, he would be hailed as a major philosopher). She was beautiful and, needless to say, the smartest girl in the class. He was attracted, and he moved. Within months they were lovers. The affair lasted four years.

Heidegger did all the controlling, Hannah did all the worshiping—naturally, how could it have been otherwise—but the dynamic between them was something of an equalizer. He needed her intelligent adoration as much as she needed to give it. They both approached his talent for thinking with reverence, each believing he was a vessel of containment for something large, something to be served, protected, and responded to always. This intensity between them, as it turned out, proved a bond stronger than either love or world history.

In the spring of 1933, Heidegger became rector at the University of Freiburg. In an infamous inaugural speech, he endorsed National Socialism and laid the university at the service of the Nazi regime. That summer Hannah Arendt left Germany. She did not return to the country of her birth for seventeen years. By the time she did, she had become a political thinker of international reputation, and Heidegger was living in poverty, in occupied Germany, with a ban on his teaching.

She told herself that she would not contact him, that February in 1950, but the minute she reached Freiburg she picked up the phone. Within hours he was at the hotel. Two days later she wrote to him,

When the waiter announced your name it was as though time had stopped. Then, in a flash, I became aware—I have never before admitted it, not to myself and not to you and not to anyone else—that the force of my impulse [to get in touch] has mercifully saved me from committing the only truly unforgivable disloyalty, from mishandling my life. But you must know one thing . . . that had I done so, it would have been out of pride only—that is, out of pure, plain, crazy stupidity. Not for any reason.

Three months later Heidegger sent her four letters in quick succession to say that her return to his life had brought him joy; that she alone was close to him when he was thinking; that he dreamed of her living nearby and of running his fingers through her hair. He sounded like a man newly charged, filled with hope and longing, excited and immensely glad to be alive.

They were both mesmerized by the reconciliation, Heidegger no less than Arendt. Afterward, of course, they were overtaken repeatedly by the people they had actually become, but to a remarkable degree each remained compelled by the other, continuing to write and meet for the next twenty-five years until 1975 when, as it happened, they died within months of one another.

～

An attachment persisted, irrationally, between two people who, by all the declared laws of social history, should have become repulsive to one another. It's the irrationality that's interesting, where the drama resides, where one interpreting guess is as good as another. The question is asked, How could she—preoccupied as she was with the ethical life—not only have continued to love a man who'd been a Nazi, but also go on, in the sixties, to argue in print that he hadn't really known what he was doing, that he was a political innocent?

Arendt's attachment to Heidegger has been traced analytically by Elzbieta Ettinger to the fact that her father died when she was seven, her mother remarried a man she detested, and the intelligent, melancholy child that was Hannah Arendt grew up fixated on the need to love a great and unavailable man who would always stand above her, arousing her to awe. She needed, Ettinger argues, to experience this kind of loss and helplessness again and again; it was her inner necessity. No sooner did she make contact with Heidegger in 1950 than she fell prey to it once more.

I, for one, am entirely persuaded by such speculation. I don't doubt that Arendt's love for Heidegger did resemble that of the anxiety-ridden child for the at first unavailable and then dead father; and I have no doubt it *did* reinforce the bundle of emotional fears and inhibitions sealed off inside the intellectual toughness that became Arendt's trademark style. But this kind of psychologizing is interesting, as the dramatists know, only when presented inside a larger mythology, one that provides an objective correlative to the uncontrollable need of the protagonist. Such a mythology Arendt and Heidegger had right to hand.

These were prototypic European intellectuals. They worshiped the act of intellection. For them, thinking was what raised man above the animals. More than raised him: made him significant, transcendent. To think well or brilliantly was to stand inside the gate of paradise; to think badly, or not well enough, was to be expelled from Eden. From this judgment there was neither escape nor dispensation. If you dreamed of living a serious life and you had no intellectual ability, you might as well not live at all. Simone Weil wanted to kill herself when she was fourteen years old because she saw, with penetrating suddenness, that she would never be as intelligent as her brother Andre.

For such people, Heidegger was a visionary, a man surrounded by an aura, imbued with the dark power of "thinking." This astonishing gift placed him, in the imagination of almost everyone who knew him, beyond ordinary judgment. To do it as *he* did it was to climb Mount Olympus. Reading him, or listening to him speak, people felt exalted. His very presence renewed the *idea* of being alive. The experience carried with it the conviction of re-creation, aroused an inner atmosphere toward which one yearned—not a sensation to be resisted. And no one did resist it. Not Hannah Arendt, not Karl Jaspers, not anyone exposed to the man whose gifts of mind were large enough to persuade that he saw life whole, and then he saw beyond.

This attachment is, essentially, a parable of the longing for transcendence. The longing is the romantic heart of the matter. It was a killer. It sank a hook in all those to whom it spoke. The hook was attached to an intensity that dragged at the heart. The question of who can free themselves when devotion threatens integrity of the self, and who cannot, is indeed a matter of temperament, understanding, and wholeness of being—that is, the freedom of action that flows from integration of mind and spirit.

The control in the story is Karl Jaspers. What Arendt saw in Heidegger, he saw too. What she felt, he felt too. He yearned for the company of Martin Heidegger's conversation. When the war was over, Jaspers thought continually of seeing his former brilliant student. The two men wrote a number of times to one another (Heidegger wanted reconciliation badly), but they never again met. Heidegger had been a Nazi who had neither repented nor apologized; that, in the end, carried more weight with Jaspers than the beloved greatness of mind. It was hard for Jaspers—when Arendt came to visit he spoke openly of his difficulty—but he was a man of integrated feeling. He understood his conflict, and he subdued it. He acted rationally.

Hannah Arendt could not avail herself of Jaspers's solution. She had been the student, not the teacher, and she had slept with Heidegger. Worship of the transcendent mind, once eroticized, can (and for her I believe it did) become a thing one bonds with somewhere in the nerve endings. Once an experience becomes fused with an irreducible sense of self—and this is inescapable—the impulse to rationalize its "contradictions" replaces the impulse to act rationally and looks, to the one doing it, like the same thing. To explain Heidegger's Nazi sympathies as harmless became a reasonable undertaking for Arendt, as reasonable as she was to herself. I understand the act perfectly. I grew up in the company of people unable to separate from the Communist Party when to stay meant to go on explaining the inexplicable, but to leave—to walk away from the only transcendence they would ever know—meant living with a granulated ache in the nerves that would tell them for the rest of their lives they'd been expelled from Eden. And this, they decided, they simply could not do. Such "decisions" are taken in a place in the psyche well below the one where rational thought operates effectively—the place that Arendt, essentially, discounted.

She never grasped the power of repressed feeling. She was a woman who froze up in the presence of openly expressed emotion and was then thrown into confusion by the response her defensive toughness elicited. That's why the tone of *Eichmann in Jerusalem* is so cold. It was the coldness for which she could not be forgiven—a response that stupefied her: couldn't they *see*, the fools, couldn't they see? No, they *couldn't* see. Any more than she could see.

Arendt scorned Freud, and she despised the American devotion to psychoanalysis. She found the talk obsessive and half-baked; it aroused in her neither interest nor empathy; she could not imagine that hidden within it were ideas reflective of a reality that mattered. The contempt was symptomatic; it sealed her off from all knowledge of her own inner conflicts. Because she was sealed off she was more vulnerable to them than another, simpler but more self-inspecting person, might have been. More vulnerable and, at last, more dramatically at fault.

⁓

Today—after thirty years of politics in the street, thirty years of the therapeutic culture, thirty years of a soul-searching civil rights movement—that historic devotion to transcendence through art and intellect feels strange, even somewhat foreign. But it is the history of shared sensibility, the thing we all felt up until yesterday. How many women and men have I, in my short, obscure lifetime, watched subjugate themselves to The Great Man, the one who seemed to embody art with a capital A or revolution with a capital R? Our numbers are legion. We ourselves were intelligent, educated, talented, none of us moral monsters, just ordinary people hungry to live life at a symbolic level. At the time, The Great Man seemed not only a good idea but a necessary one, irreplaceable and unforgettable.

We are, I think, too close to the inner events of this story to judge its meaning. But judging is our necessity—it speaks directly to our own anxieties, relieves us of the burden of ourselves. We can resist it no more than Hannah Arendt could resist Martin Heidegger.

Christina Stead

MENTION HER NAME among people who read and almost invariably a face will light up: "*The Man Who Loved Children!* An extraordinary book." Then quickly it narrows down: "I've never known what to make of her." A sentence or two more, and a growing suspicion is confirmed. Christina Stead's readers share the judgment that compares her with Ibsen and Tolstoy but recall her work with discomfort not pleasure; remember being gripped (hard) by the sentences, but not wanting to go back for more. She's like no one else, a reader will muse. The work takes hold of you, in the style of a vise not an embrace. The sentences tighten around the heart; the pressure begins to feel threatening; illumination radiates from an angry jolt. A Stead novel, it is agreed, provides the shock of recognition with the emphasis on the shock.

～

She was born—in Australia in 1902—the intelligent, ungainly child of a handsome, overbearing, story-telling father who did not love it that she grew up un-beautiful. Her mother died when Christina was a baby. Her father remarried and had six children. The father was an amazing blowhard, convinced at all times of the rightness and goodness of his own cause. He dazzled the family with the power of life in him, even as he bent it mercilessly to his will. The stepmother—weak, cunning, ambitious—was made wild by the father. They fought openly, bitterly, to the death. The children bounced off the walls so often they grew up stunned.

Christina was smart and fat. She watched, and she ate, and she listened. She never forgot any of it: not the bedlam of the marriage or her own self-defeating hunger; not the complicated exercise of her father's self-love or the crazed stepmother; not the squalor of the house or the way the world got shut out. This knot of memory burned in her, became the central experience of her writing life. Like most central experiences, it both gave her her subject and set the limits on what she would do with it.

In her early twenties she came out of Australia: lively, mercurial, unbelievably quick-witted, and in a rage. The rage was crucial. It wasn't that anger gave the work its power: anger *was* the work: the work at its astonishing best. Stead knew early on this made the writing problematic: reviewers on both sides of the Atlantic were alarmed. So she drew back (often) from the pleasure of the sparking blaze that fired in her this black, reckless, amazing language. There are twelve novels and two collections of stories. It's hard to realize the same woman wrote all those books.

In *The Little Hotel*, for instance, and in most of the stories, the prose is spare, detached, sophisticated. In *The Man Who Loved Children* the writing is electric and exhaustive, the tone of one deep in the middle of the matter, and the voice is tremendously intelligent but not at all what you'd call sophisticated. This alternation of style is there early and late, before *The Man Who Loved Children* and after it. The theory goes that because Stead's great book was largely ignored upon publication, she became demoralized and never went on to risk the electric voice again, but looking through her work as a whole, it is easier to believe that the mercurial life of her own inner promptings determined the curious back and forthness of her writing. One thing seems clear: when Stead was in the grip of her demon she wrote *The Man Who Loved Children*, and when she was released from it she wrote *The Little Hotel* and the stories. *I'm Dying Laughing* (published after her death) is the last wrestle with the demon.

The Man Who Loved Children is her masterpiece, the keystone in her arch. Here, and for the only time, she brought together control of her craft and a relentless inner concentration on that which still burned in her. It's the relentlessness that gives the book its genius. She has opened herself without stint to the way that early life felt. The way it *felt* is a swift, black tidal wave of language: one that threatens to drown the reader, but doesn't.

Inside a rambling house in suburban America, sometime during the depression, sits Henny Pollit, thin, dark, stringy, old at thirty-eight, eating herself alive on account of her rotten marriage. Six kids tumble about the house, along with a twelve-year-old stepdaughter named Louie. Feeling besieged, Henny yells at one, "Oh leave me alone, you're worse than your father." At another she snarls, "What do you mean sneaking up on me like that, are you spying on me like your father." At a third she screams, "Get out of my sight before I land you one, you creeper." Then she instructs the children to tell their father—Mr. Saint, Mr. Above-It-All, Mr. Never-Made-A-Wrong-Move—the roof is leaking. She herself does not speak to her husband.

Hardworking, conscientious Sam Pollit comes through the door into this house he considers a travesty of home, unable to believe he is locked up with a vengeful lunatic who makes his days and nights a living hell. How could this have happened to him. Him! ("He believed in himself so strongly that sure of his innocence and good intentions, he felt he was Good, and he could not do anything but good. Those who opposed him, a simple reasoning, were evil.") Sam shrugs off his unhappy thought and calls the children to him, demanding, now that he is home, that they come and play the game of life with him. The children run forward, ready to join Sam at his hard, insistent pleasure, but one among them doesn't want to play. Sam badgers and teases mercilessly until the boy bursts into humiliated tears, and rushes off to hide himself. "You have to do that, don't you?" Louie bites off at her father. Henny stands sneering in the doorway, then wrenches herself away.

We are thrust into the middle of things—what to make of these people? all of them bursting on us at once—and we are given no help. Neither tone nor narrative viewpoint reveals the writer's sympathies or intentions. The Pollits are just *there*; violently, overwhelmingly there; taking up all the air and all the space. Puzzled, disturbed, we read on. The syntax—dense, furious, unexpected—is compelling. The sentences fix us, hold us in position, while the writing drives forward.

Somewhere around page 300, the prose seems to draw back from itself and, for a moment, we are given distance on the Pollits. Louie's teacher comes to dinner and we see them as they look to the world: poor, shabby, marginal. In another moment we are plunged back into the thick of it, but too late. We've realized something important about *The Man Who Loved Children* and about Christina Stead's writing. Stead has her eye right up against the thing she is looking at because—that is the thing she is looking at. The prose itself is a black, glowering eyeball pressed against its material. There *is* no distance, that's the whole point. Therein lies the drama of the book, in this extremity. That is its shock, and its recognition.

When the tale is ended—with an event as horrifying today as on the day it was written—all the parts of the story come together, and we see the meaning of what Stead has recounted: the murderousness of ordinary family life. We turn the last page and close the book. Slowly, the tightness around the heart eases up, and the pressure begins to recede. We feel oddly released, even expanded. We realize what this book has accomplished: it has forced us to enlarge ourselves so that we might take in its hard and terrible excitement.

The Christina Stead who wrote *The Man Who Loved Children* also wrote *I'm Dying Laughing,* a novel that makes strong use of her years in the United States (the forties and fifties); and again, a novel dominated by this extraordinary syntax that burrows into the situation, tries to get a fix on things, becomes the story itself. But this novel journeys on and on yet refuses somehow to arrive.

In 1973, when she'd been working on and off at it for twenty-three years, Stead said of the book,

> It was all about the passion of—I use passion in almost the religious sense—of two people, two Americans, New Yorkers, in the thirties. They were doing well, but they suffered all the troubles of the thirties. They were politically minded. They went to Hollywood. They came to Europe to avoid the McCarthy trouble. Of course they were deeply involved. And then, they lived around Europe, oh, in a wild and exciting extravagant style. But there was nothing to support it. At the same time they wanted to be on the side of the angels, good Communists, good people, and also to be very rich. Well, of course. . . . They came to a bad end.

To begin with and to end with, the characters (Emily Wilkes and Stephen Howard) are fabulous talkers. We are in the presence of two people who howl and scream and babble endlessly but never bore themselves, each other, or the reader. Cooking eggs, taking a shit, deciding on a house, one or the other of them is delivering volumes of commentary and analysis. *I'm Dying Laughing* is a river, a torrent, an avalanche of talk. The people Emily and Stephen live among are also passionate talkers. The Communist Party sessions in New York and Hollywood—there is no more accurate imitation in American literature of the sound and feel (and length!) of that kind of talk.

But it's Emily's talk that dominates the book, Emily's talk that *is* the book. Her thoughts, her longings, her hopeless battles with herself over weight and work are what give scope and direction to *I'm Dying Laughing*. She hates herself for writing potboilers. She wants to write "serious." But she can't. Her will, her appetite, her conversation, are so remarkable they amount to a kind of genius, yet she has no capacity for serious writing. Eaten up by her dilemma, she is always hungry. So she eats. And does she eat: pages and pages of Emily bingeing and dieting interwoven with the disheveled, disorganized concerns of the house in Paris where she and Stephen live like movie stars, all the while seeing themselves as American Reds on the run.

Emily and Stephen are provided with a windup as grisly as the one given the Pollits, but it doesn't come to the same thing at all. "I meant it to go on from fire to more fiery to fierier still," Stead once said, but she knew long before she died that she had lost her way with this book; it had taken her down a road she never meant to travel; the further she went, the more lost she got; the more lost she got, the more pages of talk she accumulated.

Yet the talk is not just an amazement. The fire is banked but it *is* fire, and it *does* burn. These pages flicker and flame—the eating, the dishevelment, the manic confusion between greed and idealism—with a writer's burning need. Out of that need some awful alchemy occurs on the page beyond the reader's ability to resist.

Stead never loved her characters. She didn't scorn them either. She took an angry, involved *interest* in them: very angry, very involved. The writer (a generation ahead) whom she most resembles is Sylvia Plath. In Plath, too, rage is the organizing principle. In her, too, burns an exploding star of language, dark and violent, beside itself with the need to *go all the way*. I can see each of them at the typewriter, reeling about in the chair, both being made frantic by a headful of the unthinkable and the unsayable. Then each one takes a healthy cupful of rage, calms down, and begins to write. Sometimes a piece of work emerges whole and glorious and overpowering, sometimes not; but always on the page the electrifying syntax, the sinister rhythms, the force of inner necessity.

Grace Paley

I REMEMBER THE FIRST TIME I laid eyes on a Paley sentence. The year was 1960, the place a Berkeley bookstore, and I a depressed graduate student, leafing restlessly. I picked up a book of stories by a writer I'd never heard of and read: "I was popular in certain circles, says Aunt Rose. I wasn't no thinner then, only more stationary in the flesh. In time to come, Lillie, don't be surprised—change is a fact of God. From this no one is excused. Only a person like your mama stands on one foot, she don't notice how big her behind is getting and sings in the canary's ear for thirty years." The next time I looked up it was dark outside, the store was closing, and I had completed four stories, among them the incomparable "An Interest in Life" and "The Pale Pink Roast." I saw that the restlessness in me had abated. I felt warm and solid. More than warm: safe. I was feeling safe. Glad to be alive again.

There have been three story collections in thirty-five years. They have made Paley internationally famous. All over the world, in languages you never heard of, she is read as a master storyteller in the great tradition: people love life more because of her writing. In her own country Paley is beloved as well, but it's complicated. Familiarity is a corrective. Limitations are noted as well as virtues. The euphoria is harder earned. For many American readers, the third collection is weaker by far than the first. Scope, vision, and delivery in a Paley story seem never to vary or to advance: the wisdom does not increase: the cheerful irony grows wearisome, begins to seem folksy. Oh Grace! the critically minded reader berates a page of Paley prose, as though it were a relative. You've done this *before*. And besides, this, what you have written here, is not a story at all, this is a mere fragment, a little song and dance you have performed times without number. Then suddenly, right there, in the middle of this same page refusing to get on with it, is a Paley sentence that arrests the eye and amazes the heart. The impatient reader quiets down, becomes calm, even wordless. She stares into the sentence. She feels its power. Everything Paley knows went into the making of that sentence. The way the sentence was made *is* what she knows: just as the right image is what the poet knows. The reader is reminded then of why—even though the stories don't "develop," and the collections don't get stronger—Paley goes on being read in languages you never heard of.

⌒

No matter how old Paley characters get they remain susceptible to the promise that someone or something is about to round the corner and make them feel again the crazy, wild, sexy excitement of life. Ordinary time in a Paley story passes like a dream, embracing the vividness of remembered feeling. Age, loss of appetite, growing children, economic despair, all mount up: the "normalcy" that surrounds the never-forgotten man, moment, Sunday morning when ah! one felt intensely.

Strictly speaking, women and men in Paley stories do not fall in love with each other, they fall in love with the desire to feel alive. They are, for each other, projections and provocations. Sooner or later, of course (mostly sooner), from such alliances human difficulty is bound to emerge, and when it does (more often than not), the sensation of love evaporates. The response to the evaporation is what interests Paley. She sees that people are made either melancholy by the loss of love, or agitated by it. When agitated they generally take a hike, when melancholy they seem to get paralyzed. Historically speaking, it is the man who becomes agitated and the woman who becomes melancholy. In short, although each is trapped in behavior neither can resist and both will regret, men fly the coop and women stand bolted to the kitchen floor.

This sense of things is Paley's wisdom. The instrumental nature of sexual relations is mother's milk to the Paley narrator. She knows it so well it puts her beyond sentiment or anger, sends her into a Zen trance. From that trance has come writer's gold: the single insight made penetrating in those extraordinary sentences. Sentences brimming with the consequence of desire once tasted, now lost, and endlessly paid for. Two examples will do.

Faith Darwin—of "Faith in the Afternoon"—is swimming in misery over the defection of her husband, Ricardo. When her mother tells her that Anita Franklin, a high-school classmate, has been left by *her* husband, Faith loses it:

> Anita Franklin, she said to herself. . . . How is it these days, now you are never getting laid anymore by clever Arthur Mazzano, the brilliant Sephardic Scholar and Lecturer? Now it is time that leans across you and not handsome, fair Arthur's mouth on yours, or his intelligent Boy Scouty conflagrating fingers.
>
> At this very moment, the thumb of Ricardo's hovering shadow jabbed her in her left eye, revealing for all the world the shallowness of her water table. Rice could have been planted at that instant on the terraces of her flesh and sprouted in strength and beauty in the floods that overwhelmed her from that moment on through all the afternoon. For herself and Anita Franklin, Faith bowed her head and wept.

Now, the obverse. In "Wants" the Paley narrator runs into her ex-husband and has an exchange with him that reminds her "he had had a habit throughout the twenty-seven years of making a narrow remark which, like a plumber's snake, could work its way through the ear down the throat, halfway to my heart. He would then disappear, leaving me choking with equipment."

These sentences are born of a concentration in the writer that runs so deep, is turned so far inward, it achieves the lucidity of the poet. The material is transformed in the sound of the sentence: the sound of the sentence *becomes* the material; the material is at one with the voice that is speaking. What Paley knows—that women and men remain longing, passive creatures most of their lives: always acted upon, rarely acting—is now inextricable from the way her sentences "talk" to us. She is famous for coming down against the fiction of plot and character because "everyone, real or invented, deserves the open destiny of life," but her women and her men, so far from having an open destiny, seem hopelessly mired in their unknowing, middle-aged selves. It is the narrating Paley voice that is the open destiny. That voice is an unblinking stare; it is modern art; it fills the canvas. Its sentences are the equivalent of color in a Rothko painting. In Rothko, color *is* the painting; in Paley, voice *is* the story.

Like that of her friend Donald Barthelme, Grace Paley's voice has become an influential sound in contemporary American literature because it reminds us that although the story can no longer be told as it once was, it still needs to go on being told. The idiosyncratic intelligence hanging out in space is now the story: and indeed it is story enough. I felt safe in its presence in a Berkeley bookstore thirty years ago, it makes me feel safe today. As long as this voice is coming off the page I need not fear the loss of the narrative impulse. I need not, as Frank O'Hara says, regret life.

Tenderhearted Men

THERE'S A CERTAIN KIND of American story that is characterized by a laconic surface and a tight-lipped speaking voice. The narrator in this story has been made inarticulate by modern life. Vulnerable to his own loneliness, he is forced into an attitude of hard-boiled self-protection. Yet he longs for things to be other than they are. He yearns, in fact, for tender connection. Just behind the leanness and coolness of the prose lies the open but doomed expectation that romantic love saves. Settings vary and regional idioms intrude, but almost always in these stories it is men and women together that is being written about.

Fifty years ago the strongest version of this story was written by Ernest Hemingway. Today, it survives in the work of Raymond Carver, Richard Ford, and Andre Dubus. One enormous difference obtains between the earlier writer and the later ones. Hemingway held an allegorical view of life that idealized women as the means of spiritual salvation, then condemned them as agents of subversion. Raymond Carver, Richard Ford, and Andre Dubus are neither sexists nor misanthropes. On the contrary: tenderness of heart is their signature trait. These men share an acute sense of the compatriot nature of human suffering. Their women are fellow victims.

Nevertheless, from Hemingway to Andre Dubus, what is striking to a reader like myself is the extraordinarily fixed nature of what goes on between characters who are men and characters who are women. The narrator invariably subscribes to an idea of manhood that hasn't changed in half a century, and the women he knows seem to subscribe similarly. Their relations are the irreducible in the writing, the immutable circumstance from which the writer pulls his wisdom, his truth, his story. This sense of men and women struggling together in dumb erotic need supplies Hemingway's three successors with the central metaphor. It arouses in each of them an astonishing capacity to respond to the desolation of ordinary lives in modern times. It gives them a strength of despair from which their powers derive. And it leaves me with the taste of ashes in my mouth.

~

There's a small Carver story called "Are These Actual Miles?" that illustrates perfectly what I mean. Toni and Leo are married. Leo has gone bankrupt. All that remains is the red convertible bought in the good years. Toni is being sent out to sell the car for the best price she can get. She leaves the house, dressed to kill, at four in the afternoon. Leo sits waiting for her return. Just after nine, she calls to say the sale is almost completed. He hears music in the background. "Where are you?" he asks nervously. After a bit more conversation, she hangs up. A while later she calls again: Any minute now, honey. "Come home," he pleads. She hangs up. Two or three hours later, another call. He's frantic. At dawn she comes in drunk, with the check in her purse. He looks at her. "Bankrupt!" she screams, and passes out. Leo puts her to bed. After a while, he gets in beside her. Here are the final lines of the story:

> Presently he reaches out his hand and touches her hip. . . . He runs his fingers over her hip and feels the stretch marks there. They are like roads, and he traces them in her flesh. He runs his fingers back and forth, first one, then another. They run everywhere in her flesh, dozens, perhaps hundreds of them. He remembers waking up the morning after they bought the car, seeing it, there in the drive, in the sun, gleaming.

Her stretch marks, his convertible: it comes finally to that. The story, like much of Carver's fiction, is permeated with the nakedness of the moment. This is Carver's great strength: stunning immediacy, remarkable pathos. No other American writer can make a reader feel, as he does, right up against it when a character experiences loss of hope. It is impossible to resist the power of such writing, and while I'm reading the story I don't. But then I find myself turning away. The atmosphere congeals.

I feel manipulated. These people fail to engage me. I cannot be persuaded that life between Toni and Leo was good when the convertible stood gleaming in the driveway. What's more, I don't think Carver thinks life was good then, either. I think he yearns to believe that it *should* have been good, not that it actually was. This yearning is the force behind his writing. What fuels the intensity of his gaze, the clarity with which he pares down the description, is not a shrewd insight into the way things actually are between this man and this woman but a terrible longing to describe things as they might have been—or should have been. The sense of loss here is original and primal, unmediated by adult experience.

Connection between people like Toni and Leo is predicated on the existence of a world in which men and women conform to a romantic notion of themselves as men and women. These two have never been real to each other. They were bound to end in her stretch marks, his convertible. Carver knows that. Instead of being jolted by what he knows, startled into another posture, he feels only sad and bad. He mourns the loss of romantic possibility in each life; in Carver's work, story after story—"What Do You Do in San Francisco?" "Gazebo," "They're Not Your Husband," "Little Things," "What We Talk About When We Talk About Love"—is saturated in a wistful longing for an ideal, tender connection that never was, and never can be. Carver's surrogate character seems always to be saying, "Wouldn't it be lovely if it could have been otherwise?" In short, the work is sentimental. Trapped inside that sentimentality is the struggle so many women and so many men are waging now to make sense of themselves as they actually are. The struggle has brought men-and-women-together into a new place; puzzling and painful, true, but new nonetheless. In the country of these stories not only is that place not on the map, it's as though the territory doesn't exist.

⌣

There's a novel by Richard Ford in which the narrating protagonist says, "Women have always *lightened* my burdens, picked up my faltering spirits and exhilarated me with the old anything-goes feeling though anything doesn't go, of course, and never did. . . . [But now] . . . I have slipped for a moment out onto that plane where women can't help in the age-old ways. . . . Not that I've lost the old yen, just that the old yen seems suddenly defeatable by facts, the kind you can't sidestep—the essence of a small empty moment." Frank Bascombe delivers himself of this insight on page 61 of *The Sportswriter* and then goes on speaking until page 375 exactly as though he hadn't. Taking in his own experience is not what this man is about.

Frank came to New York in his twenties, from an anonymous American life that included Mississippi and the Midwest, because he'd written a book of stories that promised to commit him to a life of literature. But New York terrified him, and he couldn't keep up the writing. So he got married, became a sportswriter, and moved to the suburbs. Frank tells us all this as though he himself is puzzled as to how this drastic turn of events came about. "I had somehow lost my sense of anticipation at age twenty-five," he offers by way of explanation. "And I had no more interest in what I might write next than I cared what a rock weighed on Mars."

It's emblematic of the book that Frank, now thirty-eight and divorced, can't figure out why things have turned out as they have, and finds his own ignorance strange and dreamy. "Dreamy" is his euphemism, the word he uses to describe the way he feels about almost everything: the end of serious writing, the death of his son, the breakup of his marriage, the love affairs that come to nothing. New York saddens him unbearably, and New Jersey gives him rest and relief. Everything else makes him dreamy.

Frank Bascombe's depression is Richard Ford's weakness. Ford is in love with it. It is responsible for the tenderness he bears the men in his stories, nearly all of whom are drifters, pained and bewildered people driven by their own sad emptiness into proto-typic American violence. Here, in *The Sportswriter*, Ford has abandoned dialect, so to speak, but the commuter and the drifter are the same man: lonely, confused, hurting. Especially con-fused. It's the bewilderment that touches Ford deeply. Frank's not knowing what is happening to him is the story Ford is tell-ing—life inflicting itself on the most ordinary of men.

But there is so much Frank Bascombe *could* understand, and seems not to *want* to understand, that it is hard to trust his pain. For example, his perpetual dreaminess about the women in his life is unpersuasive. The novel begins with an affair. Frank tells us that he loves the dating ritual and that Vicki, a nurse from Texas, loves to let him love it. He also tells us that it is in Vicki's nature to put her faith "more in objects than in essences. And in most ways that makes her the perfect companion." Then he tells us that he longs to run away with Vicki, to marry her and bliss out forever on her good-natured sexiness. Ford allows Frank to mock himself, to parody his own expectations of love, but Vicki is so unremittingly a fantasy that this entire episode seems only peculiar. The man who daydreams this kind of rescue is, somehow, not credible.

At the end of the novel, Frank has another affair of a few months' duration, this time with a college girl who spends a summer at the magazine he works for. Toward the end of this one, Frank observes, "I doubt ours is a true romance. I am too old for her; she is too smart for me. . . . I . . . have also been pleased to find out she is a modern enough girl not to think that I can make things better for her one way or another, even though I wish I could." Not true. He doesn't wish it at all. It's only errant wistfulness drowsing through him.

Between these two affairs, the novel gives us summarized evocations of other women Frank has slept with, or failed to sleep with. These women are spoken of in the way that we all speak of people who once caused sexual infatuation to bloom in us: not as real in themselves, reminders only of the aliveness we have felt in passion.

It is inconceivable in *The Sportswriter* that a person who is a woman should strike Frank simply as a familiar, as another human being floating around in the world, lost, empty, shocked to the bone by the way it's all turned out. He feels compassion for women but not empathy. At bottom, they do not remind him of himself. The only character in the book who even comes close is his ex-wife, and she, incredibly enough, is called X. It is X who brought on the divorce, X who found the emptiness between them unbearable, X who wanted to take another stab at living her life and, although she looks like a busy suburban mother, X too seems to be floundering and suffering. We can only deduce this from the hints Frank throws out. We never see X straight on. She is a shadowy figure, always at the periphery of Frank's vision. One would assume that he would know her well. But he doesn't. She is the ex-wife. In his mind, the people who embody his condition are other men he runs up against in a random fashion. There are these men, who are like himself, and then there are the women, who can no longer give comfort against the overwhelming force of life.

Andre Dubus, the most complex and least well known of the three, is the most articulate in the matter of men-and-women-together. A writer who yearns for Roman Catholicism, loves the Marines, and suffers over the loss of permanence in marriage, Dubus makes the metaphor reach with as much ambition as did Hemingway. For nearly twenty years, he has been writing stories and novellas that are filled with this preoccupation. It runs like a continuous current beneath the surface of his prose, providing his work with force and direction, and sometimes taking the work down to a place where the waters are still, and very deep indeed. His is among the strongest writing now being done in American fiction. The strength both compels and disturbs, as the work describes with transparency a condition of life it seems, almost self-consciously, to resist making sense of.

Dubus's characters—blue-collar people who live in the old mill towns not far from Boston—are mechanics, waitresses, bartenders, and construction workers. They have almost no conversation in them, and very little sense of things beyond their own immediate needs. They drink, they smoke, they make love: without a stop. Inevitably, the limitation of appetite becomes apparent, and they begin to suffer. When they suffer, they do terrible things to themselves, and to one another. There is nothing any of them can do to mitigate the suffering. They cannot educate themselves out of their lives; they can't leave home, and they can't get reborn. This situation is Dubus's subject, the thing he concentrates on with all his writer's might. His concentration is penetrating. We feel his people trapped in their lives so acutely that they enter into us.

The sympathetic detachment he brings to bear on the failure of marriage to lessen the emptiness of soul lying in wait for his characters is Dubus's strongest quality. It is there in some of his best work: in the novel *Voices from the Moon*, as well as in the novellas *Adultery* and *We Don't Live Here Anymore*, where the working class is deserted for a set of characters drawn from Dubus's own life. But working class or middle class, the people in these stories all suffer relentlessly from the same terrible surprise. It's the surprise one feels most vividly. This failure of marriage has been a central experience for Dubus, one that seems to have come unexpectedly and with a jolt. The shock and the immensity of it remain with him.

In *Adultery*, Hank and Edith meet as graduate students in Iowa. He's serious, she's not. He works passionately to make himself a writer; she only wants to be the girl he loves. They marry, have a child, and for Edith the years pass in contentment. Hank, meanwhile, is being eaten up by his life: he grows hungrier by the day, restless and ambitious for he knows not what. He begins an affair. Edith faces him down. He denies nothing. In fact, he tells her he doesn't believe in monogamy. She is astonished and frightened. "Why didn't I ever know any of this?" she says. "You never asked," he replies. He tells her to calm down; he says he loves her and wants to continue as a family. Only now, he adds, things are out in the open; there's no going back to their old way of being together. Edith is stricken, but she feels helpless. She agrees to an openly adulterous marriage: he will have lovers, she will have lovers. Five years pass. Then Edith takes as a lover a forty-year-old man who has just left the priesthood. She's the only woman Joe Ritchie has ever slept with. Joe is shocked by her marriage. He tells her she is living in sin, and if she stays with Hank she'll "grow old in pieces." Slowly, she comes to see her life as her lover sees it. Within the year, Joe begins to die of cancer. Edith nurses him. Now, as he nears death, she is repelled by her marriage. She tells Joe she is divorcing her husband.

The genius lies with having given the story to Edith: it is from inside her thoughts and feelings that we read. She—the untried, girlish woman—is the blank slate on which to write the grief, rage, and humiliation of modern marriage. It is Edith who will best register the cost to the human spirit, Edith who can instruct the reader in what it feels like to make an unholy alliance, Edith who makes your skin crawl.

Adultery is not a plea for the return of old-fashioned monogamous marriage; it is only a description of one kind of spiritual hell. Because marriage means so much to Dubus, he is able to use its corrupted form to describe the dictates of the human heart under vile circumstances in perilous times. This novella is his masterpiece. It is also a blueprint for his fundamental text on men and women together.

There's a scene in *Adultery* in which Edith observes her husband at a party. Here's a bit of what she's thinking:

> Edith watched Hank, and listened to him. Early in their marriage she had learned to do that. His intimacy with her was private; at their table and in their bed they talked; his intimacy with men was public, and when he was with them he spoke mostly to them, looked mostly at them, and she knew there were times when he was unaware that she or any other woman was in the room. She had long ago stopped resenting this; she had watched the other wives sitting together and talking to one another; she had watched them sit listening while couples were at a dinner table and the women couldn't group so they ate and listened to the men. Usually men who

talked to women were trying to make love with them, and she could sense the other men's resentment at this distraction, as if during a hand of poker a man had left the table to phone his mistress. Of course she was able to talk at parties; she wasn't shy and no man had ever intentionally made her feel he was not interested in what she had to say; but willy-nilly they patronized her. As they listened to her she could sense their courtesy, their impatience for her to finish so they could speak again to their comrades. . . . [She saw that] Hank needed and loved men, and when he loved them it was because of what they thought and how they lived. He did not measure women that way; he measured them by their sexuality and good sense. He and his friends talked with one another because it was the only way they could show their love. . . . It no longer bothered her. She knew that some women writhed under these conversations; they were usually women whose husbands rarely spoke to them with the intensity and attention they gave to men.

In Dubus's work, sexual love is entirely instrumental. Men and women are alive to themselves and to one another only in the mythic way. They provoke in themselves the fantasy that romantic love will bring one to safe haven. They are tremendously influenced by an idea of "men" and an idea of "women" that Ernest Hemingway would have understood and approved of, but that many people today find alarming, if not downright silly. The reader can see early on that the marriage in *Adultery* will come to disaster. Without genuine connection—that is, connection of the mind or spirit—sexual feeling quickly wears itself out. Such love is bound to come a cropper. Yet neither Dubus nor his characters see what the reader sees. In many of his stories, the characters are middle-aged and have been through these affairs many times over. Yet they remain devoted to the fantasy. They resist taking in their own experience. Theirs is the distress of people unable to arrive at wisdom.

Behind Hank and Edith (and Hank's future girlfriends) stand the young men and women in Dubus's Marine stories and his loss-of-virginity stories. Here young men elevate the mystique of physical courage into an idea of manhood that, today, seems puzzling, and young women develop a concern for virginity that is equally off-putting. Even if the models for these stories still exist—and, of course, they do, in the tens of thousands—they are, in some large sense, no longer plausible. They seem to occur in a vacuum of history. What Dubus has to say in these stories is so emotionally unconvincing that, even though he writes the same good prose he always does, and one reads every sentence with interest, the work loses power.

To create characters who are themselves unknowing is one thing; to write as though you know only as much as your characters know is another. In these stories, there is no distance at all between character and narration. Dubus seems to be at one with these young men and women. He is soaked in nostalgia, even as they are, for an idea of men and women together that is evaporating now—and, for many of us, can't dry up fast enough.

But Dubus doesn't want that idea to go. When we get to his

Catholicism, we see how deeply he does not want it to go, and we see even more clearly what lies behind the poetic toughness of his writing.

In "A Father's Story," we have a man speaking from inside the middle of his life. He's divorced, a devout Catholic who will not remarry; he lives alone on a horse farm, his only friend the local priest. Slowly, he tells us about last summer, when his twenty-year-old daughter was visiting him. One evening she went out with friends. On her way back, driving alone at one in the morning, she hit a man. The man's body went flying across the road. The girl pushed down on the gas pedal and fled. When she arrives home, she tells her father what she's done and he, seeing how terrified she is, decides to shield her. He drives back over the road and finds the body. For one awful minute, he thinks it's breathing; he decides to leave it anyway. He drives home, takes the daughter's car into town and drives it into a tree in the priest's front yard to conceal its already broken headlight. At the end of this account, the narrator speaks with God:

> I do not feel the peace I once did: not with God, nor the earth, or anyone on it. . . . [But now] in the mornings . . . I say to Him: I would do it again. For when she knocked on my door, then called me, she woke what had flowed dormant in my blood since her birth, so that what rose from the bed was not a stable owner or a Catholic . . . but the father of a girl.
>
> And He says: I am a Father too. . . .
>
> True. . . . And if one of my sons had come to me that

night, I would have phoned the police and told them to meet us with an ambulance at the top of the hill.

Why? Do you love them less?

I tell Him no, it is not that I love them less, but that I could bear the pain of watching and knowing my sons' pain, could bear it with pride as they took the whip and nails. But You never had a daughter and, if You had, You could not have borne her passion.

So, He says, you love her more than you love Me.

I love her more than I love truth.

Then you love in weakness, He says.

As You love me, I say, and I go with an apple or carrot out to the barn.

"A Father's Story" moves forward under the influence of a disturbing piece of social, if not religious, orthodoxy—God is to man as man is to woman—akin to the sense of things that lies behind the Marine and loss-of-virginity stories. It posits, in Catholic terms, a hierarchy of existential vulnerabilities that mythicizes men, women, love, and the mystery of life. It is hard to know what Dubus is wanting to say with such a conceit, especially now, when so many women and men are struggling to meet at eye level, to extend a hand across the open ditch that surrounds each of our lives. Who among us is to be moved or comforted by the assurance that we are *all* as children commended to the care and pity of a Fatherly Being, but that, still, only a son need bear the consequences of his act?

Life is a Christian drama for Dubus's characters precisely

because they understand so little about themselves in a world where self-understanding has become crucial. These people are bewildered, they act badly and are held accountable. Nevertheless they are innocent. This, for Dubus, is religious metaphor: from it he derives his strength. Damnation mesmerizes him, holds his full attention, compels his deepest response. He may not have very much more understanding than his characters do of why their lives grow empty, but the emptiness itself he feels brilliantly: the look and the taste of it, the anguish it causes and the compromised inner peace to which it leads.

In Dubus's work, as in that of Carver and Ford, strength of feeling for the desolation in American life has brought new vitality to the kind of story that is famous for a hard surface beneath which spreads a contained flood of sentiment. But inside that tender toughness these stories have always seemed to be asking, "Why aren't things the way they used to be?" And, essentially, that's what they're still asking.

The despair of these writers can never be as moving to a reader like me as it is to the writers themselves. At the heart of their work lies a keen regret that things are no longer as they once were between men and women, a regret so intense that it amounts to longing. It's this longing, endowed with the appearance of hard reality, that informs much of their writing. But from where I stand, the hard reality is this: that question about why things are not as they once were has got to be asked honestly, not rhetorically. Then something more might be known about why life is so empty now, and the work of writers as good as Andre Dubus, Raymond Carver, and Richard Ford would be wise as well as strong.

The End of the
Novel of Love

WHEN I WAS A GIRL the whole world believed in love. My mother, a communist and a romantic, said to me, "You're smart, make something of yourself, but always remember, love is the most important thing in a woman's life." Across the street Grace Levine's mother, a woman who lit candles on Friday night and was afraid of everything that moved, whispered to her daughter, "Don't do like I did. Marry a man you love." Around the corner Elise Goldberg's mother slipped her arms into a Persian lamb coat and shrugged, "It's just as easy to fall in love with a rich man as a poor man," and she meant it. Love was the operative word.

It was a working-class, immigrant neighborhood in the Bronx. Most of our homes were marked by an atmosphere of emotional indifference, if not open antagonism. I don't think I ever walked into a house where I felt the parents loved each other, or had once loved each other. I knew early that the people around me had married out of a set of necessities stronger than the absence of passion. Still, everyone believed in love. *Our* lives might be small and frightened, but in the ideal life, it was felt—the educated life, the brave life, the life out in the world—love would not only be pursued, it would be achieved; and once achieved transform existence; create a rich, deep, textured prose out of the ordinary reports of daily life. The promise of love alone would one day give us the courage to leave these caution-ridden precincts and turn our faces toward: experience. That was it, really. Love, we knew, would put us at the center of our own experience. In fact, only if we gave ourselves over to passion, without stint and without contractual assurance, would we *have* experience.

Oh yes, we in the Bronx knew that love was the supreme accomplishment. We knew it because we, too, had been reading *Anna Karenina* and *Madame Bovary* and *The Age of Innocence* all our lives, as well as the ten thousand middlebrow versions of those books, and the dime-store novels too. We knew it because we lived in a culture soaked through with the conviction that love had transforming powers: to know passion was to break the bonds of the frightened, ignorant self. There might, of course, be a price to pay. One might be risking the shelter of respectability if one fell in love with the wrong person, but in return for such loss one would be gaining the only knowledge worth having. The very meaning of human risk was embedded in the pursuit of love.

We in the Bronx believed as we did because for a hundred and fifty years in the West the idea of romantic love had been emblematic of the search for self-understanding: an influence that touched every aspect of the world enterprise. In literature, good and great writers alike sounded depths of thought and emotion that made readers feel the life within themselves in the presence of words written to celebrate the powers of love.

I remember the first time—it wasn't so long ago—I turned the last page of a novel and it came over me that love as a metaphor was over. The book was Jane Smiley's *The Age of Grief*. I'd thought it a fine piece of work, resonant with years of observation about something profound, but it struck me as a small good thing, and I remember sitting with the book on my lap wondering, Why only a small good thing? Why am I not stirred to a sense of larger doings here? Almost immediately I answered myself with, Love is the problem here. It's the wrong catalyst. It doesn't complicate the issue, it reduces it. My own thought startled me. I'd never before considered that love might dilute the strength of a good novel rather than gather it in.

The situation in *The Age of Grief* is that of a couple in their thirties who've been together ten or twelve years, living in some small city, the parents of three little girls. The narrating voice is that of the husband: grave, intelligent, trustworthy. One winter night, he tells us, driving home from a church concert in which the wife has performed—he at the wheel with one of the children beside him, she in back with the other two—he hears her say, "I'll never be happy again." He looks at her face in the rear-view mirror. Suddenly he knows that she is having an affair, and all he wants is that she not confess.

What follows then is a wonderfully told tale of the months of family life that pass as the husband hopes to avert open crisis, and the wife wanders about like a sick cat, trying to muddle silently through her own sadness and suppressed desire. The climax occurs when the entire family falls ill with the flu and the husband sees them through so beautifully, so decently, that you, the reader, could weep, reading his scrupulous recapitulation of the fever that has at last overtaken them all. The day after the last child recovers, the wife bolts. And then she returns.

The genius of the narrative lies in the desperate calm with which the husband charts the weeks and months of unhappy suspicion, all the while a piece of unwanted knowledge is collecting steadily in him. "I am thirty-five years old," he tells us in the middle of his story, "and it seems to me that I have arrived at the age of grief. Others arrive there sooner. Almost no one arrives much later. . . . It is not only that we know that love ends, children are stolen, parents die feeling that their lives have been meaningless. . . . It is more that . . . after all that schooling, all that care . . . the cup must come around, cannot pass from you, and it is the same cup of pain that every mortal drinks from." There. He has said what he came to say, and said it quite clearly.

The final paragraph reads: "Shall I say I welcomed my wife back with great sadness, more sadness than I had felt at any other time? It seems to me that marriage is a small container, after all, barely large enough to hold some children. Two inner lives, two lifelong meditations of whatever complexity, burst out of it and out of it, cracking it, deforming it. Or maybe it is not a thing at all, nothing, something not present. I don't know, but I can't help thinking about it."

The situation is worthy of Tolstoy or Flaubert or Wharton—a pair of protagonists moving into the long littleness of life, falling into chaos when one of them jerks in the wind for a moment, refusing to accommodate the stasis ahead—and while Jane Smiley may not have the skills of the masters, her gifts are nonetheless considerable. Yet, for me, *The Age of Grief* failed to grow large. The story moved me to sadness and regret, but it could not persuade me to the tragic or the inevitable. I found myself arguing with its premises.

It was necessary that I believe the wife is driven to risk all for an experience that promises to give her back a self she has failed to achieve in her marriage; but the conviction that such knowledge would be hers if she went off with the man she was now burning for refused to exert power over me. As the novella progressed I saw that I was thinking, If this woman leaves her husband for her lover, in six months she'll be right back where she started. There isn't a reason in the world to believe she will know herself any better with the second man than she does with the first. This passion of hers is a quick fix, a soporific. We've all been through it a thousand times. She's foolish to think love will save her. I certainly don't.

And then again, I thought, If she *does* go off, what is she actually risking? When Emma Bovary was loosening her stays with a man other than her husband, or Anna Karenina running away from hers, or Newbold Archer agonizing over whether to leave New York with Ellen Olenska, people were indeed risking all for love. Bourgeois respectability had the power to make of these characters social pariahs. Strength would be needed to sustain exile. Out of such risk taking might come the force of suffering that brings clarity and insight. Today, there are no penalties to pay, no world of respectability to be excommunicated from. Bourgeois society as such is over. If the wife in *The Age of Grief* walks away from her marriage, she'll set up housekeeping on the other side of town with a man named Jerry instead of one named Dave, in ten minutes make a social life the equivalent of the one her first marriage had provided her, and in two years she and her new husband will find themselves at a dinner party that includes the ex-husband and his new wife: everyone chatting amiably. Two years after that, one morning in the kitchen or one night in the bedroom, she'll slip and call Jerry Dave, and they will both laugh.

For this character to be hungering for erotic passion at a crucial moment when she's up against all that she has, and has not, done with her life struck me as implausible. She *had* to know better, I thought. On the other hand, if blissing-out was what the wife was up to, then the story could be made large only if the author of her being called her on it. But Jane Smiley wasn't calling her on it. She was using the illicit passion of the wife straight— as though she expected me, the reader, to accept erotic longing

at face value as an urgency compelling enough to bring into relief the shocking ordinariness of these stricken lives. But I did
not accept it. I could not. I know too much about love. We *all*
know too much. I could not accept as true that a love affair would
bring the wife (and therefore me) to feel deeply the consequence of her original insufficient intentions. And that is why an
otherwise excellent novella struck me as a small good thing. Embedded as it was in a convention, not a truth, the conceit itself
prevented the writer from asking the questions necessary to
deepen thought and action.

Only forty years ago most of us occupied a world remarkably free
of direct experience. We grew up expecting to repeat our parents' lives; certainly, we repeated their platitudes. However
much some of us may have acted the girl or the boy of advanced
ideas, we all (secretly or otherwise) subscribed to Aristophanes'
fable: somewhere out there was our fated "other half," the one
true love that would rescue us from loneliness and drift. This expectation was central to our lives: what is otherwise known as a
self-fulfilling prophecy.

When love-and-marriage failed to deliver us to the promised
land within, we became sad, angry, confused. We thought we'd
been cheated. We still believed in love but clearly: you could
make a mistake. You could take Wrong for Right, and then marriage not only failed to rescue, it became existential hell.

There was, of course, always divorce, but forty years ago

nobody *we* knew got divorced. We'd also heard about psycho-analysis (from movies and novels), but in the Bronx such treatment was taken as proof of irredeemable defeat—hardly a legitimate search for relief from the confusion in which many of us were passing our lives. As yet, there was nothing for it but to endure. We became fond of responding to irony in novels of love as one would to a finger pressed against the flesh near an open sore.

Good writers, of course, had the boldness to deliver border reports from the country of married sadness and anger, and these reports were received with morbid excitement. In the fifties John Cheever's stories of marital disillusion seemed profound. That famous climactic moment in Cheever when the husband *realizes* his wife holds him in contempt, or the wife *knows* the husband is committing adultery, these moments delivered an electric charge. The knowledge encoded in them seemed literally stunning, leaving the characters riven, their lives destroyed. Who, after all, could go on after this? Then came the shocker—the thing that made the story large, awesome, terrible—they *did* go on like this. The reader came to the last sentence and sat staring into space, the void opening at her feet.

The world was changing but it was not yet changed; that's why Cheever's stories had such power. Great-love-and-lasting-marriage was still the expectation upon which lives were predicated; until the moment the expectation dissolved out, it seemed immutable. We were living Cheever's stories, but we did not know how to make any larger sense of things than he had made of them.

Then, within a generation, everything everywhere in the world conspired to *make* us know. Suddenly, there *was* divorce. And psychotherapy. And sex and feminism and drugs, as well as crime in the street. In short, it was the Fall of Rome. From one end of the city to the other. Even in the Bronx. Frightening, but exciting as well. We who had married for life were reprieved: at liberty to correct the mistake. We would fall in love again, and this time we'd do it right. *Now* we would discover ourselves, emerge into the fine, free creatures we had always known we could be. We got divorced, and we went into therapy. And this is what happened:

We loved once, and we loved badly. We loved again, and again we loved badly. We did it a third time, and we were no longer living in a world free of experience. We saw that love did not make us tender, wise, or compassionate. Under its influence we gave up neither our fears nor our angers. Within ourselves we remained unchanged. The development was an astonishment: not at all what had been expected. The atmosphere became charged with revelation, and it altered us permanently as a culture.

A couple of years ago, at dinner with a couple I've known for years—he is an academic, she a poet; he makes the money, she does not—I fell into some aimless exchange about marriage, in the middle of which the husband had occasion to announce casually, "Of course, it's a given that the one who does the supporting holds the one being supported in contempt." The wife stared at him. He stared back. Then she gasped, "Henry! I can hardly believe you've said what you've just said." He looked at her, unperturbed. "What is it?" he asked mildly. "Is this something we don't all know?" Silence fell on the company. She looked bleak, he remained impassive. A minute later she said the equivalent of Pass the salt. I remember thinking, If life was still a Cheever story this would have been the climactic moment, but as it is now 1995 it is only a break in the conversation.

Henry was speaking a hard, simple truth we have all absorbed. Love, this truth tells us, like food or air, is necessary but insufficient: it cannot do for us what we must do for ourselves. Certainly, it can no longer act as an organizing principle. Romantic love now seems a yearning to dive down into feeling and come up magically changed; when what is required for the making of a self is the deliberate pursuit of consciousness. Knowing *this* to be the larger truth, as many of us do, the idea of love as a means of illumination—in literature as in life—now comes as something of an anticlimax. If in a story (as in actuality) neither the characters nor the narrator realizes, *to begin with*, that love is not what it's all about, then the story will know at its conclusion only what it knows at the beginning. Such a tale may establish sorrow and sentimental regret, but it cannot achieve a sense of the tragic or the inevitable. The panic with which people discover that the life they are living is the only one they are able to make—this panic cannot be addressed if the major event in the story is going to be a new affair.

It is not that thousands of people aren't doing exactly what the husband and the wife in *The Age of Grief* are doing—of course they are, every hour on the hour. It is, rather, that their situation no longer signifies. It cannot provide insight, it can only repeat a view of things that today feels sadly tired and without the power to make one see anew. Somewhat like a going-nowhere analysis in which we recite again and again what we have repeatedly failed to act on. Such failure transforms insight into ritual. Ritual sustains the status quo. When a patient repeats an insight ritually he is living in bad faith: without intentionality: in thrall to passive longing. When a writer sits down to tell a tale based on experience that in effect has become "ritual," it is the equivalent of living in bad faith.

In great novels we always feel that the writer, at the time of the writing, knows as much as anyone around can know, and is struggling to make sense of what is perceived somewhere in the nerve endings if not yet in clarified consciousness. When a novel gives us *less* than many of us know—and is content with what is being given—we have middlebrow writing. Such writing—however intelligent its author, however excellent its prose—is closer to the sentimental than to the real. The reader senses that the work is sentimental because the metaphors are inaccurate: approximate, not exact. To get to those nerve endings a metaphor must be exact, not approximate. The exact metaphor is writer's gold.

A hundred years ago love provided such gold. When Lawrence, James, Stendhal, were writing, readers felt themselves in the presence of men diving down into the depths. For these writers love was a snake pit, marriage a menacing drama. Their insights were penetrated through with anxiety, their stories accumulated dread. Love, then, provided the context within which an enormous amount could and did get said. The writing promised self-understanding—that alone which gives courage for life—and it delivered.

Even fifty years ago—when most of us occupied a world free of experience—it could still deliver, and at the hands of writers who were good not great. In 1950, Rosamond Lehmann—in the 1930s she had been Jane Smiley's English counterpart—wrote a novel in which the central situation is that of a man who falls in love with a pair of sisters. He marries one, and within a few years begins sleeping with the other. This story, at the time of the writing, struck readers as bold, thrilling, dramatic. I picked the book up a few years ago, ready to experience a literary curiosity, but I found the novel strong and memorable. Lehmann had made of the situation a remarkable context for the weakness of human intensity, and had let her characters live long enough to see that each of their lives had taken shape around the weakness. A novelist formed in a time when love was everything had used love to explore fully a flash of true insight. I turned the last page feeling penetrated by the pitiableness of life.

Could this book have been written today? Never. Its power is wholly dependent on the static quality of the world against which its characters are struggling. Everything they learn and do and become takes place against that restraint. It is because they cannot get out that the intensity builds and they break the taboo. The broken taboo allows them into themselves. That is how the story deepens.

Put romantic love at the center of a novel today, and who could be persuaded that in its pursuit the characters are going to get to something large? That love is going to throw them up against themselves in such a way that we will all learn something important about how we got to be as we are, or how the time in which we live got to be as it is. No one, it seems to me. Today, I think, love as a metaphor is an act of nostalgia, not of discovery.